MW00716968

Becoming a
Woman
God Can Use

Becoming a *Woman* God Can Use

Lessons From God's Female Board Of Directors

Andrea Rose Butler

TATE PUBLISHING *& Enterprises*

Published by Tate Publishing & Enterprises, LLC
127 E. Trade Center Terrace | Mustang, Oklahoma 73064 USA
1.888.361.9473 | www.tatepublishing.com

Tate Publishing is committed to excellence in the publishing industry. The company reflects the philosophy established by the founders, based on Psalm 68:11,
"The Lord gave the word and great was the company of those who published it."

Book design copyright © 2008 by Tate Publishing, LLC. All rights reserved.
Cover design by Kandi Evans
Interior design by Summer Floyd-Harvey

Published in the United States of America

ISBN: 978-1-606096-298-5
1. Christian Living
2. Inspiration: Motivational
08.09.17

Table of Contents

Introduction

Becoming a woman that God can use is not the Wonder Woman syndrome where we feel that we have to be it all and do it all. It is more than just a woman who is busy and encumbered and overwhelmed with doing. She is focused on a set goal. I believe that we have all been caught in the snare of doing and doing and yet not finding fulfillment. We have been told the lie that if we go to all the right schools, obtain the right education, marry the right man, and have two-point-five children, then all should be well. We have achieved it all.

Yet we find our lives unfulfilled. We move from one relationship to another. We change jobs. We try to find the perfect house. We diet to lose weight so that we can look like the perfect ten. Yet all of that has failed, and we are left wondering if there is more to the life that we live. However, the life that we seek cannot be obtained outside of a relationship with the Creator. We are instructed to "Seek first the Kingdom of God, and His righteousness and all these things will be added to us" (Matthew 6:33 KJV).

As we begin our study, it is important to note that in order to move forward and have the life that you want to live, "the abundant life," you must first enter into a relationship with God through the redemptive work of Jesus Christ.

As we share throughout our time of study, we will discover the importance of relationship, how our life experiences are needed for the work of the kingdom of God, and that nothing that you have experienced was for naught. You will see and decide what you want God to do with your pain, your praise, and your victory. As we come together, we will learn through shared experiences how to be used by God and network with others to reach our destiny.

So come on, let's grow together as we become women whom God can use.

God Bless You!

ANDREA

A Call to Relationship

The Want Ad

*D*o you know that you are wanted? That God needs you? That He cannot fulfill His divine call without you? You may think that God does not notice or want you. That you have done some terrible things that you cannot be forgiven for, but God has sent out an advertisement where He is looking for you. In John 3:16–17 we read, "For God so loved the world that He gave his only begotten Son that whosoever believes on Him [Jesus] should not perish but have everlasting life. God did not send His Son into the world to condemn the world, but that through Him all the world might me saved"(TAB). Do you fall into the category of whosoever? Then this call is to you as well.

The Importance of Relationship

*W*hy is it important that we enter into a relationship with Christ? I am glad you asked. Let me give an illustration that we as women can relate to. Have you ever reached into your cupboard to pull out a glass or cup only to realize as you begin to pour that the object is dirty with some stuck-on food or stains. That cup or glass there on the shelf looked clean; it was there on the shelf waiting but not available for use. Now you would not want to drink out of that glass or cup. You are on a mission. The kids are crying; they are hungry or you, yourself may be thirsty. You really don't have time to wash it out. So what do you do? You reach into the cupboard and get another one.

The same is true with God; He is looking for vessels that are clean and fit for his immediate use.

Maybe He has already been calling out to you. He has tried to use you, but you were not ready to surrender, and He had to put you away. He has been trying to clean you up; however, you keep moving away from the cleansing work that He has been trying to do in you. Time is short. The fields are white unto harvest and God is looking for vessels that He can use to bring in that harvest (John 4:35; Matthew 9:37). You won't always have time to repent, so today is the acceptable year of the Lord.

> After reading the above statement, why is it important for you to have a relationship with God?
>
> READ JOHN 15:1–8.

_____

_____

_____

After reading the above verses, has your opinion of the importance of having a relationship with God changed?

_____

_____

_____

If yes—What about your opinion changed and why?

_____

_____

_____

If no—What did you understand the passage to mean?

_____

_____

_____

Steps to a Relationship

*I*f you are ready to take that all-important step, it is as easy as ABC. A step that we can take together:

> A—Admit that you are a sinner and that you cannot save yourself: "For all have sinned and fall short of the glory of God" (Romans 3:23, NIV) and "For the wages of sin is death, but the gift of God is eternal life in Christ Jesus our Lord"
>
> (ROMANS: 6:23, NIV).

B—Believe in your heart that Jesus died on the cross to take the penalty for your sins and that He was raised from the dead to make intercession for you: "That if you confess with your mouth, 'Jesus is Lord,' and believe in your heart that God raised

Him from the dead, you will be saved" (Romans 10:9, NIV).

C—Confess with your mouth the Lordship of Jesus over your life: "For it is with your heart that you believe and are justified, and it is with your mouth that you confess and are saved" (Romans 10:10, NIV).

_____

_____

_____

_____

_____

_____

Prayer of Repentance: Lord Jesus, I admit that I am a sinner and that I cannot save myself. I know that I need you, Jesus, to be the Lord and savior of my life. I accept what you did on the cross as full payment for all my sins. I know that it is through your grace that I am saved and not by any works that I can do. I surrender my will and my life over to you. I thank you for your free gift of eternal life; come and live in me now. In Jesus' name, amen!

Beginning Your New Life

Read your Bible daily—Start with the book of John (2 Timothy 2:15; Joshua 1:8).

Prayer—Spend time talking to God; He loves to hear from you (Luke 18:1; Ephesians 6:18; 1 Thessalonians 5:17).

Worship—Spend time with other believers in a church setting (Hebrews 10:23–25).

Fellowship—Spend time with other believers. "As iron sharpens iron, so a man sharpens the countenance of his friend." (Proverbs 27:17).

Witness—Tell others about the change in your life (Acts 1:8; Matthew 28:19, 20).

Andrea Rose Butler

"But may all who seek you rejoice and be glad in you; may those who love your salvation always say, 'Let God be exalted.'"

PSALM 70:4, NIV

Notes

A Call to the Available

The Interview

You have seen the advertisement; you have responded by entering into a relationship with God through His son, Jesus. He now has your resume in hand and it has been reviewed, and God Himself has determined that you are the woman for the job. In Ephesians 2:10 we read, "You are God's own handiwork (His workmanship), recreated in Christ Jesus [born anew], that we may do those good works which God predestined (planned beforehand) for us (taking paths which He prepared ahead of time), that we should walk in them [living the good life, which He prearranged and made ready for us to live] (TAB). He has reviewed every trial that you have overcome, your pain, your wounds, and your response in the midst of those trials. Every time you have been wounded (spiritually, emotionally, and physically), He has determined how He may use all those skills and work them together for your good and His glory (Romans 8:28). His next question is, when are you available to start working?

Job Availability

*H*ave you ever gone on a job interview, and the interviewer asked that all-important question, "When are you available?" and you had to pull out your calendar and figure out when the best time for you was? You thought about all the arrangements you would have to make: childcare, how late you would be getting home, how early you had to get up; would this job interfere with your social life? Would you have to travel? All these thoughts were running through your head, but you knew how desperately you wanted or needed this job. You knew that you had to get on with your life. The thoughts are always there. What would I have to give up? In addition: What's in it for me? To answer these questions, let's take a look at what Scripture has to say about this.

Read: Mark 10:17–31

What did Jesus tell the man to do, and why do you think that he was disappointed by what he was told to do?

_____

_____

_____

Why do you think the disciples asked, "Who then can be saved?"

_____

_____

_____

What does Jesus say to those who are willing to give up all to follow Him?

_____

_____

_____

Read: Mark 8:35–37

What does Jesus say about when we surrender our lives and fears to him?

Notes

_____

_____

_____

_____

_____

_____

_____

_____

_____

_____

_____

_____

_____

_____

_____

_____

Do You Have What it Takes?

*D*uring the interview you maybe asked, "Why should we hire you?" or "What makes you a more qualified candidate?" Your mind is racing. You think, Because I am desperate. On the other hand, you may think, Because I really need this job. I have been searching for a long time, and you were the first to grant an interview. However, you may be like the rich young ruler and think, I am the best candidate for this job. Did you see my resume? You need me.

Whatever your thoughts, what the interviewer really wants to know is, If we hire you, how will you advance the global interest of this company. Likewise, God awaits your answer.

Read: Romans 12:4–13 and Titus 2:3–5

List the different gifts mentioned in Romans and be prepared to discuss how we each have varying degrees of them.

_____

_____

_____

Explain how the writer says that we should treat our gifts?

_____

_____

_____

What do you believe is your gift that God can use? If you are unsure, list some things that you are good at doing.

_____

_____

_____

List some life experiences or training that you have that someone may benefit from.

_____

_____

_____

Describe an experience that you have had that you would be willing to share the life lesson learned with someone else.

_____

_____

_____

Prayer: Father, in the name of Jesus, I thank you for every trial that I have endured. Today I ask that you would take and use them for your glory. I know that I am able to do all things through Christ who gives me strength. I trust him today to work in me and to work all things together for me. Today I surrender my will and my life to his care. Amen.

Notes

_____

_____

_____

_____

_____

_____

_____

_____

_____

_____

_____

_____

_____

_____

_____

_____

_____

_____

"Thy word have I hid in mine heart, that I might not sin against thee."

PSALM 119:11, KJV

A Call to Be Faithful

*I*n our society being a faithful person is a rare commodity. People are always looking for the angle. What's in it for me? The divorce rate is the highest it has ever been in our history, and people who work less but demand higher wages. "Rules are made to be broken" is the mantra of the day and time that we live in. Yet within us there is that need to find someone or something that we can rely on. So it is with God. He is looking for a wise and faithful steward whom He can work through. Jesus tells several parables or stories about people who are faithful and those who are not. Let's examine what it means to be faithful as we explore what is found in Scripture to determine what God is looking for in the ones He has chosen to do his work.

Webster's Dictionary defines faithful as being "steadfast in allegiance (firm adherence to whatever one owes allegiance), loyal (firm resistance to any temptation to desert or betray), constant (stresses continuing firmness of emotional attachment without strict obedience to promise), and staunch (fortitude and resolution in adherence and imperviousness to influences that would weaken it)."

Faithless is defined as not being true to an allegiance or duty, false, disloyal, treacherous; any failure to keep a promise or pledge or any breach in allegiance or loyalty. In which category do you currently find yourself? Will Christ return to find you faithful or faithless?

Read: Luke 16:10–12

A Matter of Talent

Read: Matthew 25:14–30

We are told that each one was given a gift to use. How did each one regard what was given to him?

_____

_____

_____

We are told that two of the stewards increased what was given to them. Through what Pat Robertson in his book The Secret Kingdom defines as the "The Law of Use," what does that say about what we should do with what we are given?

There is the saying, "Use it or lose it!" What does that imply?

_____

_____

_____

The one with the most talent was also given more than he had accumulated on his own.

_____

_____

_____

What do you understand about how God feels when we use what He has given us?

_____

_____

_____

Explain how God felt about the excuse of the steward who was given one talent?

_____

_____

_____

Does God see fear as an excuse not to be obedient? Explain why not?

_____

_____

_____

List some obstacles that you may have.
In light of what we read concerning the stewards, how should we respond to God's calling on our lives?

_____

_____

_____

Prayer: Father, in the name of Jesus, I admit that I am fearful about what it is that you want me to do. I am even afraid that I might not be up to the task, but now by faith I will step out and trust you. Your Word says that without faith it is impossible to please you and that if I would just believe, then nothing shall be impossible for me. Thank you, Lord, for taking away any fear or anxiety that I might have. I trust you today to do the impossible through me. Amen.

Notes

_____

_____

_____

_____

_____

_____

_____

_____

_____

_____

_____

_____

_____

_____

_____

_____

_____

"Be strong and courageous. Do not be afraid or terrified because of them, for the LORD your God goes with you; he will never leave you nor forsake you."

DEUTERONOMY 31:6, NIV

Counting the Cost

*I*t is said that no one goes into battle without first counting the cost. No one purchases a home without first finding out whether he or she can afford to live there. In the Scriptures, we also learn that everything that we do has a consequence, and so we are admonished to take a look at the two sides of every situation. As we discussed earlier, Jesus said, "No one who gave up everything would not also receive in this life and in the life to come everlasting life" (Mark 10:29, 30). Without faith we came to understand that we couldn't please God. We also discussed that fear is not an excuse. So what is the cost of following Christ and being used by him to make an impact on our homes, our communities, our city, state, country, or the world?

Worthy of Life

Read: John 12:24–26

Explain what Jesus said we should do and why is it necessary?

_____

_____

_____

If we are to fulfill the call of Christ on our lives, it will require a sacrifice. Name one thing that you would find difficult to let go of in order to fulfill your purpose. Why?

_____

_____

_____

Read: Luke 14:28–33

Explain why we should be informed about the task that we are to undertake?

_____

_____

_____

Explain why is it necessary to seek wise counsel before we undertake our mission.

_____

_____

_____

Explain why we should know what resources we possess before stepping out.

_____

_____

_____

Prayer: Father, in the name of Jesus, I thank you that you have counted me worthy to work for you and to do your will. Help me not to become weary in doing good, knowing that in due season I will reap if I do not lose heart or give up. Help me to know that whatever I give up to you is not in vain, so I lay all my stuff down at your feet and call it loss that I may gain you. Amen.

Notes

_____

_____

_____

_____

_____

_____

_____

_____

_____

_____

_____

_____

_____

"The Sovereign LORD is my strength; He makes my feet like the feet of a deer, He enables me to go on the heights."

HABAKKUK 3:19, NIV

Are You Teachable?

Sheep and Goats

*J*esus tells the parables of His return when He
will do the separating of the people who say
that they are his. He will separate them into two
categories, sheep and goats. It is said that a shepherd has a staff and a rod; a staff for leading and
a rod for correction. He will use the staff to guide
the sheep, and if the sheep will not heed instruction, he will then take the rod and break its leg, and
then he will carry the sheep around his neck until
the sheep learns his voice and scent. Goats, on the
other hand, are very stubborn and rebellious. They
will turn against the herder if he tries to correct and
will not respond to any form of instruction. Jesus

says, "My sheep know my voice and a stranger, they will not follow ..." (John 10:4–5).

Read: Matthew 25:31–46

Explain why the people will be separated into categories.

_____

_____

_____

Why is it important that we use our gifts and resources wisely?

_____

_____

_____

What important lesson can we learn from this parable?

_____

_____

_____

Read: Proverbs 13:16–18 and Proverbs 16:20

Why is it important to heed instruction?

_____

_____

_____

Prayer: Father, in the name of Jesus, help me to learn the lessons that I need to so that I can graduate and go on to what you would have me do. Those times when I am stubborn, help me to yield to what you are doing in and around me. Help me to trust the plans that you have for me today and tomorrow. Lord, I want to be teachable. I ask for your help and guidance today. Amen!

Notes

_____

_____

_____

_____

_____

_____

_____

_____

_____

_____

_____

_____

_____

_____

_____

_____

_____

_____

_____

_____

_____

_____

_____

"As a prisoner for the Lord, then, I urge you to live a life worthy of the calling you have received."

EPHESIANS 4:1, NIV

The Vineyard Awaits

Fields Are White unto Harvest

Now that I know what God wants me to do, what do I do? You may be asking this question. Well, Jesus says that there is a vast field ready to be harvested, but there are no laborers to do the work. We may not all be called to be missionaries to some distant land, but is there a neighbor who may need you? What about that story you heard on the news? Somebody should help those people. Could that somebody be you? That little girl down the street who looks to you as a big sister but you have never had time for? Isn't it about time you did have time for her? If you are not connected to a local church, get hooked up and find out how your gifts and talents may be utilized. If you are in a local church and you are warming the pews, it's time to get up and get active. The ministry that I am now involved in started many years ago out of a need that I had as a single parent just recently divorced and trying to find my way. It has since grown and expanded beyond anything that I could have imagined.

> What need do you have in your life that you have said, "I wish there was _____?" Or "I wish someone would do_____!" List your need or needs.

> Think of resources that you would need to meet your need(s). List them here.

> Who would need the services that would be provided?

_____

_____

_____

What obstacles would need to be overcome?

Do some research on your own. What would it take to get started?

Get out there and start doing!

Prayer: Father, in the name of Jesus, you said that the harvest was truly great and that the laborers were few and that we were to pray to the Lord of the harvest, so now, Lord, I come to you as a laborer. I am willing to work in your vineyard. I ask for your favor with officials, creditors, agencies, and whomever I need to contact. I ask that you would give me wisdom and that my steps would be ordered by you. I ask also that you would set up divine appointments for me. Help me to keep my ears and heart open to hear your voice as you lead. Thank you for choosing and using me. Amen.

Notes

_____

_____

_____

_____

_____

_____

_____

_____

_____

_____

_____

_____

_____

_____

_____

_____

"Does not the potter have the right to make out
of the same lump of clay some pottery for noble
purposes and some for common use?"

ROMANS 9:21, NIV

Loving and Learning from God's Female Board of Directors

King Solomon wrote that "there is no thing new under the sun" (Ecclesiastes 1:9); therefore the God who worked in the lives of these ancient women is more than willing to do the same in your life. Let us look at the feminine approach God used and the lessons we can learn about loving and learning from God's Female Board of Directors.

These women were from different socio-economic and racial backgrounds; they were princesses, businesswomen, and homemakers. They varied in age and life experiences, yet God worked unbelievable miracles on the inside, which produced divine promise on the outside. They found themselves in situations that seemed humanly impossible to overcome, yet overcome they did, to leave us a legacy of faith, courage, and strength. They remind us that through Christ we can achieve all things, "for it is God who works in you to will and to act according to His good purpose" (Philippians 2:13, NIV).

Working Women

Not Just a Job but a Ministry

Priscilla

Teacher, Tent Maker

*P*riscilla and her husband, Aquila, labored together making tents, and wherever they went they would find other tent makers, and there they would share their faith in Jesus. The first husband and wife missionary team, they traveled with Paul on several of his journeys. They demonstrate for us that we can use the job that we have now and still be an example before people. Priscilla was not focused on her needs but learned vital lessons, which she passed on. She was able to use tact and wisdom to instruct others in the way of the Lord.

Read: Acts 18:1–3, 18–19, 24–26, and Romans 16:3–4.

If you are married, how can you and your husband work together to make a difference in your home, church, and/or community?

_____

_____

_____

How can you use the knowledge and skills gained from your work/career to make an impact in the kingdom of God?

Notes

_____

_____

_____

_____

_____

_____

_____

_____

_____

_____

Lydia

Business Woman, Community Leader

Lydia was a professional businesswoman; she owned her own home, which was very uncommon for women of her time. She was not ashamed of letting everyone know how she felt about her Lord. She even opened up her home to be used as a place of worship and a stopping place for Paul when he journeyed there. Lydia shows us that whatever position we hold in society, God still wants us to use those things that He has given us as a platform to touch lives. If we are faithful in the little, we can be rulers over much.

Read: Acts 16:13–15

In what way can you use your occupation as a way to reach others for Christ?

_____

_____

_____

Notes

_____

_____

_____

_____

_____

_____

_____

_____

_____

_____

_____

_____

_____

_____

_____

_____

_____

_____

_____

_____

_____

_____

_____

_____

_____

_____

_____

_____

_____

"I am a wonder and a surprise to many, but you
are my strong refuge."

PSALM 71:7, TAB

Courageous Women

Trusting God in Difficult Times

Rahab

Grace under Fire

Rahab the Harlot is one of my favorite characters in Scripture because she gives us such an awesome picture of the grace and mercy of God. Here is a woman with a checkered past, yet wherever she is mentioned in Scripture, what she did remains with her. You may think that because of your past history God cannot use you effectively. When you do think about Rahab the harlot. Here is a woman despised by those in her community because of the choices that she had to make. Yet in a time of crisis, she rescued the spies, saved her household from destruction, and ended up in the genealogy of Christ despite all that she had done.

She is forever immortalized as Rahab the harlot.

Read: Joshua 2:1, 6–9, 12–14, 6:17, 22–25; Matthew 1:5; Hebrews 11:31, and James 2:25.

Are you still haunted by the things that you have done in your past?

_____

_____

_____

If yes! Why and in what way?

_____

_____

_____

If no! Why not?

_____

_____

_____

What things, if any, would be a hindrance to you in sharing your life lesson? Why/why not?

_____

_____

_____

How can you use your past failures and mis-
takes to make an eternal difference in someone
else's life?

Notes

_____

_____

_____

_____

_____

_____

_____

_____

_____

_____

_____

_____

Esther

Taking a Stand

Esther was a teenager when she became queen of one of the most powerful empires. She was an orphan who was adopted by her cousin. She was in exile and a minority. She could have viewed her circumstances from a place of defeat, even when she learned that her people were to be destroyed; she could have hid behind her position, her age, her background, but she decided to take a stand, and because of that choice, she is heralded as a heroine. She, through her exercise of courage and strength of character, paved the way for us that no matter our situation or station, we can make a difference.

Read: Book of Esther 2:7–10, 15, 17; 4:10–16; 7: 1–3.

Name a situation that you could have changed had you taken a stand.

_____

_____

_____

What could you have done differently?

_____

_____

_____

Given the choice today and the experiences that you have had, do you believe that you would or could act differently? Why/why not?

Notes

_____

_____

_____

_____

_____

_____

_____

_____

Deborah

Warrior Wife

Now here is a woman with a unique role. She was a judge and leader of men in a time when women had no rights to be heard and were often considered to be at the same level as dogs. Yet God chose to raise her up, due to her wisdom, to settle disputes between the people. She became a voice to speak life and victory to her people while they were in a place of captivity. Therefore, even though you may live in a time or place where you are not considered to be of any importance, in God's eyes you can make an eternal difference.

Read: Judges 4:4–9, 14.

Do you see yourself as a leader?

_____

_____

_____

If yes, in what way?

_____

_____

_____

If no, why not?

_____

_____

_____

What are some characteristics of a "good" leader?

_____

_____

_____

Of the traits listed above, which ones do you possess?

_____

_____

_____

List some ways that you can speak "life" into a
person, i.e., friends, family, co-workers, or even
the cashier at the grocery store.

Notes

_____

_____

_____

_____

_____

_____

_____

_____

_____

_____

_____

_____

_____

_____

_____

_____

_____

_____

" … Skillful and godly wisdom shall enter your
heart, and knowledge shall be pleasant to you."
PROVERBS 2:10, TAB

Women Waiting to Exhale

Overcoming Extreme Relationships

Tamar

Overcomer

*T*amar's is the story of an overcomer. She was married to a man who the Bible called wicked. He dies, she marries again, he, too, is wicked, and he, too, also dies. Now she is a young widow; her father-in-law did not do what he was required by the law to do, so Tamar resorted to deceit and incest to secure her future. Though she committed a grave sin, she is regarded as righteous and is listed in the lineage of Jesus. She, too, shows us that God is able to use us even with our sinful nature to bring about his plans.

Read: Genesis 38 and Matthew 1:3.

Name a time that someone in whom you had placed your trust disappointed you.

_____

_____

_____

How did you overcome your disappointment?

_____

_____

_____

Have you learned to trust others despite what was done to you?

Notes

_____

_____

_____

_____

_____

_____

Ruth–Faithful Outcast

Ruth's story is one of disappointment and loss. She is a young woman whose husband dies, yet she feels that she should leave her homeland and follow her mother-in-law. She was once married to a wealthy man, and now she is desolate and has to do the work of a servant working in the fields. Through it all, she is faithful to her mother-in-law, who is bitter over the loss of her two sons and her husband; she is in a land where she is despised because of her heritage as a Moabitess. Through her hard work and faithfulness, she is able to restore her mother-in-law and is listed in the ancestry of Jesus. She leaves us the example that though those who should be closest to us reject us, our attitude of love and faithfulness will not go unrecognized, and through that we are able to impact lives for generations.

Read: Book of Ruth 1:12–18, 2:4–13, and 4:13–17.

Ruth had to deal with disappointment and loss. Can you imagine? She has dreamed of being a wife and mother, yet her husband dies and leaves her childless. All her hopes went to the grave with her husband.

Have you had a dream that you had to lay to rest? How did you deal with the loss or disappointment?

_____

_____

_____

_____

_____

_____

Ruth was given a second chance to have her dream, but in order to do that, she had to leave the land of her disappointment and come to a place of promise. For this exercise begin a journal and divide the journal into two sections. In the first section write the label, "My Disappointments," and in the second section write the label, "My Victories."

Notes

_____

_____

_____

_____

_____

_____

_____

_____

_____

_____

_____

_____

Naomi

A Change of Heart

Naomi is an example of how God is able to redeem us even when we turn our backs on him due to life circumstances. Naomi left her homeland a wife and mother of two sons; her future was secure, and she was protected. Then tragedy struck her husband, and both sons died suddenly. Everything that she had placed her trust in failed her. In her day women needed men for their protection, safety, and livelihood. She was lost. She became so embittered by her grief that she changed her name from Naomi, which means "pleasant," to Mara, which means "bitter." She believed that by changing her name she could alter her destiny.

Despite her emotional condition, she was used to mentor Ruth and orchestrate her marriage to Boaz and thus restore her life and bring about redemption for a nation and for eternity through Christ.

Read: Book of Ruth 1:3–5, 19–21, and 3:1–6.

Describe a situation that made a dramatic change in your life whether it was good or bad.

_____

_____

_____

How did your change affect someone else's life?

_____

_____

_____

Did that effect bring that person closer to God or drive him or her away?

_____

_____

_____

What life lessons did you learn?

_____

_____

_____

If it had a negative effect on your life, have you allowed God to heal you?

_____

_____

_____

Why/why not?

_____

_____

_____

Notes

_____

_____

_____

_____

_____

_____

_____

_____

_____

_____

_____

_____

_____

_____

_____

_____

_____

_____

"Discretion shall watch over you, understanding shall keep you."

PROVERBS 2:11, TAB

Women of Faith

Believing God Will Do the Impossible

Sarah

Age is Not a Factor

Sarah, the mother of faith, did not see her age as a thing to be despised. When she was passed childbearing age, she believed what God had promised and was able to have a child in her 90s. Though I don't recommend this, it is still possible to become pregnant with a promise, a dream, and an idea and then give birth to it. Sarah leaves us the legacy that though things may seem impossible, even dead to us, God is still able to bring new life. God is faithful to what he has promised us, and if there is a desire within us, and we trust him with it, He will bring it to pass if we don't give up.

Read: Genesis 11:29–12:20, 21:6–7.

Have you ever laughed at God's possibility for you?

Notes

_____

_____

_____

_____

_____

_____

_____

_____

_____

_____

_____

_____

_____

_____

_____

Mary–Handmaiden of God

Mary, the mother of Jesus—now, if there were ever a situation that seemed impossible, this is it. You are a teenage girl who is a virgin, and someone comes to you, an angel no less, and says you are going to have a baby and you will not have sexual relations with a man; it's just going to happen. What faith you must have to believe that! Yet happen it did, and Mary leaves us this wonderful legacy of faith as she says, "Behold your handmaiden, may it be done just as you have said" (Luke 1:38). Could you be that calm when God places a desire in your heart that seems so farfetched that no one would believe you? You are finding it hard to believe yourself. Do you have that kind of faith to say, "Here I am, Lord, and may it happen just as you have spoken"?

Read: Luke 1:26–38, 39–45.

What dream or desire has God put in your heart that you thought was impossible?

_____

_____

_____

What steps are you taking to realize that dream?

_____

_____

_____

Notes

_____

_____

_____

_____

_____

_____

_____

_____

_____

_____

_____

_____

_____

_____

_____

"When she speaks her words are wise and kindness is the rule when she gives instruction."
PROVERBS 31:21, THE BOOK

Selected — Bible Readings

A Word from the Author

*P*aul wrote to his son in the Lord, Timothy, "Study to show yourself approved unto God, a workman that needeth not to be ashamed, rightly dividing the word of truth" (2 Timothy 2:15, KJV). The Amplified version states that we should, "correctly analyze and accurately divide [rightly handling and skillfully teaching] the word of truth." By choosing to include several Bible translations for our time together, it is my hope that you will gain a deeper understanding of God's Word as we study the various ways the same Scripture is translated. Therefore, whether you are a new believer or a seasoned veteran of God's Word, you will be challenged to grow in knowledge and that the, "Eyes of your understanding may be enlightened; that ye may know what is the hope of his calling..."

EPHESIANS 1:18.

I am the true vine, and my Father is the gardener. He cuts off every branch in me that bears no fruit, while every branch that does bear fruit, he prunes so that it will be even more fruitful. You are already clean because of the word I have spoken to you. Remain in me, and I will remain in you. No branch can bear fruit by itself; it must remain in the vine. Neither can you bear fruit unless you remain in me.

I am the vine; you are the branches. If a man remains in me and I in him, he will bear much fruit; apart from me you can do nothing. If anyone does not remain in me, he is like a branch that is thrown away and withers; such branches are picked up, thrown into the fire and burned. If you remain in me and my words remain in you, ask whatever you wish, and it will be given you. This is to my Father's glory, that you bear much fruit, showing yourselves to be my disciples.

JOHN 15:1–8 (NIV)

I AM the True Vine, and My Father is the Vinedresser. Any branch in me that does not bear fruit [that stops bearing] He cuts away (trims off, takes away); and He cleanses and repeatedly prunes every branch that continues to bear fruit, to make it bear more and richer and more excellent fruit. You are cleansed and pruned already, because of the word, which I have given you [the teachings I have discussed with you]. Dwell in me, and I will dwell in you. [Live in me, and I will live in you.] Just as no branch can bear fruit of itself without abiding in (being vitally united to) the vine, neither can you bear fruit unless you abide in me. I am the Vine; you are the branches. Whoever lives in me and I in him bears much (abundant) fruit. However, apart from me [cut off from vital union with Me] you can do nothing. If a person does not dwell in me, he is thrown out like a [broken-off] branch, and withers; such branches are gathered up and thrown into the fire, and they are burned. If you live in me [abide vitally united to Me] and my words remain in you and continue to live in your hearts, ask whatever you will, and it shall be done for you. When you bear (produce) much fruit, My Father is honored and glorified, and you show and prove yourselves to be true followers of mine.

JOHN 15:1–8 (TAB)

I am the true vine, and my Father is the husbandman. Every branch in me that beareth not fruit he taketh away: and every branch that beareth fruit, he purgeth it, that it may bring forth more fruit. Now ye are clean through the word, which I have spoken unto you. Abide in me, and I in you. As the branch cannot bear fruit of itself, except it abide in the vine; no more can ye, except ye abide in me.

I am the vine, ye are the branches: He that abideth in me, and I in him, the same bringeth forth much fruit: for without me ye can do nothing.

If a man abides not in me, he is cast forth as a branch, and is withered; and men gather them, and cast them into the fire, and they are burned.

If ye abide in me, and my words abide in you, ye shall ask what ye will, and it shall be done unto you.

Herein is my Father glorified, that ye bear much fruit; so shall ye be my disciples.

JOHN 15:1–8 (KJV)

As Jesus started on his way, a man ran up to him and fell on his knees before him. "Good teacher," he asked, "what must I do to inherit eternal life?"

"Why do you call me good?" Jesus answered. "No one is good—except God alone. You know the commandments: 'Do not murder, do not commit adultery, do not steal, do not give false testimony, do not defraud, honor your father and mother.'" "Teacher," he declared, "all these I have kept since I was a boy." Jesus looked at him and loved him. "One thing you lack," he said. "Go, sell everything you have and give to the poor, and you will have treasure in heaven. Then come, follow me."

At this the man's face fell. He went away sad, because he had great wealth. Jesus looked around and said to his disciples, "How hard it is for the rich to enter the kingdom of God!" The disciples were amazed at his words. But Jesus said again, "Children, how hard it is to enter the kingdom of God! It is easier for a camel to go through the eye of a needle than for a rich man to enter the kingdom of God."

The disciples were even more amazed, and said to each other, "Who then can be saved?" Jesus looked at them and said, "With man this is impossible, but not with God; all things are possible with God."

Peter said to him, "We have left everything to follow you!"

"I tell you the truth," Jesus replied, "no one who

has left home or brothers or sisters or mother or father or children or fields for me and the gospel will fail to receive a hundred times as much in this present age (homes, brothers, sisters, mothers, children and fields—and with them, persecutions) and in the age to come, eternal life. But many who are first will be last, and the last first."

MARK 10:17–31 (NIV)

And as He was setting out on His journey, a man ran up and knelt before Him and asked Him, Teacher, [You are essentially and perfectly morally] good, what must I do to inherit eternal life [that is, to partake of eternal salvation in the Messiah's kingdom]?

And Jesus said to him, why do you call me [essentially and perfectly morally] good? There is no one [essentially and perfectly morally] good—except God alone.

You know the commandments: Do not kill, do not commit adultery, do not steal, do not bear false witness, do not defraud, honor your father and mother.

And he replied to Him, Teacher, I have carefully guarded and observed all these and taken care not to violate them from my boyhood.

And Jesus, looking upon him, loved him, and He said to him, You lack one thing; go and sell all you have and give [the money] to the poor, and you will have treasure in heaven; and come [and] accompany Me [walking the same road that I walk].

At that saying the man's countenance fell and was gloomy, and he went away grieved and sorrowing, for he was holding great possessions.

And Jesus looked around and said to His disciples, with what difficulty will those who possess wealth and keep on holding it enter the kingdom of God!

And the disciples were amazed and bewildered and perplexed at His words. But Jesus said to them again, Children, how hard it is for those who trust (place their confidence, their sense of safety) in riches to enter the kingdom of God!

It is easier for a camel to go through the eye of a needle than for a rich man to enter the kingdom of God.

And they were shocked and exceedingly astonished, and said to Him and to one another, Then who can be saved?

Jesus glanced around at them and said, with men [it is] impossible, but not with God; for all things are possible with God.

Peter started to say to Him, Behold, we have yielded up and abandoned everything [once and for all and joined You as Your disciples, siding with

Your party] and accompanied you [walking the same road that You walk].

Jesus said, Truly I tell you, there is no one who has given up and left house or brothers or sisters or mother or father or children or lands for my sake and for the Gospel's.

Who will not receive a hundred times as much now in this time—houses and brothers and sisters and mothers and children and lands, with persecutions—and in the age to come, eternal life.

But many [who are now] first will be last [then], and many [who are now] last will be first [then].

MARK 10:17–31 (TAB)

And when he was gone forth into the way, there came one running, and kneeled to him, and asked him, Good Master, what shall I do that I may inherit eternal life?

And Jesus said unto him, Why callest thou me good? There is none good but one, that is, God.

Thou knowest the commandments, Do not commit adultery, Do not kill, Do not steal, Do not bear false witness, Defraud not, Honour thy father and mother.

And he answered and said unto him, Master, all these have I observed from my youth.

Then Jesus beholding him loved him, and said unto him, One thing thou lackest: go thy way, sell whatsoever thou hast, and give to the poor, and thou shalt have treasure in heaven: and come, take up the cross, and follow me.

And he was sad at that saying, and went away grieved: for he had great possessions.

And Jesus looked round about, and saith unto his disciples, How hardly shall they that have riches enter into the kingdom of God!

And the disciples were astonished at his words. But Jesus answereth again, and saith unto them, Children, how hard is it for them that trust in riches to enter into the kingdom of God!

It is easier for a camel to go through the eye of a needle, than for a rich man to enter into the kingdom of God.

And they were astonished out of measure, saying among themselves, who then can be saved?

And Jesus looking upon them saith, with men it is impossible, but not with God: for with God all things are possible.

Then Peter began to say unto him, lo, we have left all, and have followed thee.

And Jesus answered and said, Verily I say unto you, there is no man that hath left house, or brethren, or sisters, or father, or mother, or wife, or children, or lands, for my sake, and the gospel's,

But he shall receive an hundredfold now in this

time, houses, and brethren, and sisters, and mothers, and children, and lands, with persecutions; and in the world to come eternal life.

But many that are first shall be last; and the last first.

MARK 10:17–31 (KJV)

For whoever wants to save his life will lose it, but whoever loses his life for me and for the gospel will save it. What good is it for a man to gain the whole world, yet forfeit his soul? Or what can a man give in exchange for his soul? If anyone is ashamed of me and my words in this adulterous and sinful generation, the Son of Man will be ashamed of him when he comes in his Father's glory with the holy angels."

MARK 8:35–37 (NIV)

For whoever wants to save his [higher, spiritual, eternal] life, will lose it [the lower, natural, temporal life which is lived only on earth]; and whoever gives up his life [which is lived only on earth] for My sake and the Gospel's will save it [his higher, spiritual life in the eternal kingdom of God].

For what does it profit a man to gain the whole world, and forfeit his life [in the eternal kingdom of God]?

For what can a man give as an exchange (a compensation, a ransom, in return) for his [blessed] life [in the eternal kingdom of God]?

MARK 8:35–37 (TAB)

For whosoever will save his life shall lose it; but whosoever shall lose his life for my sake and the gospel's, the same shall save it.

For what shall it profit a man, if he shall gain the whole world, and lose his own soul?

Or what shall a man give in exchange for his soul?

MARK 8:35–37 (KJV)

Just as each of us has one body with many members, and these members do not all have the same function, so in Christ we who are many form one body, and each member belongs to all the others. We have different gifts, according to the grace given us. If a man's gift is prophesying, let him use it in proportion to his faith. If it is serving, let him serve; if it is teaching, let him teach; if it is encouraging, let him encourage; if it is contributing to the needs of others, let him give generously; if it is leadership, let him govern diligently; if it is showing mercy, let him do it cheerfully. Love must be sincere. Hate what is evil; cling to what is good. Be devoted to one another in brotherly love. Honor one another above yourselves. Never be lacking in zeal, but keep your spiritual fervor, serving the Lord. Be joyful in hope, patient in affliction, faithful in prayer. Share with God's people who are in need. Practice hospitality.

ROMANS 12:4–13 (NIV)

For as in one physical body we have many parts (organs, members) and all of these parts do not have the same function or use, So we, numerous as we are, are one body in Christ (the Messiah) and individually we are parts one of another [mutually dependent on one another].

Having gifts (faculties, talents, qualities) that differ according to the grace given us, let us use them: [He whose gift is] prophecy, [let him prophesy] according to the proportion of his faith;[He whose gift is] practical service, let him give himself to serving; he who teaches, to his teaching;

He who exhorts (encourages), to his exhortation; he who contributes, let him do it in simplicity and liberality; he who gives aid and superintends, with zeal and singleness of mind; he who does acts of mercy, with genuine cheerfulness and joyful eagerness.

[Let your] love be sincere (a real thing); hate what is evil [loathe all ungodliness, turn in horror from wickedness], but hold fast to that which is good.

Love one another with brotherly affection [as members of one family], giving precedence and showing honor to one another.

Never lag in zeal and in earnest endeavor; be aglow and burning with the Spirit, serving the Lord.

Rejoice and exult in hope; be steadfast and patient in suffering and tribulation; be constant in prayer.

Contribute to the needs of God's people [sharing in the necessities of the saints]; pursue the practice of hospitality.

ROMANS 12:4–13 (TAB)

For as we have many members in one body, and all members have not the same office: So we, being many, are one body in Christ, and every one members one of another.

Having then gifts differing according to the grace that is given to us, whether prophecy, let us prophesy according to the proportion of faith; Or ministry, let us wait on our ministering: or he that teacheth, on teaching; Or he that exhorteth, on exhortation: he that giveth, let him do it with simplicity; he that ruleth, with diligence; he that sheweth mercy, with cheerfulness.

Let love be without dissimulation. Abhor that which is evil; cleave to that which is good. Be kindly affectionate one to another with brotherly love; in honour preferring one another; Not slothful in business; fervent in spirit; serving the Lord;

Rejoicing in hope; patient in tribulation; continuing instant in prayer; distributing to the necessity of saints; given to hospitality.

ROMANS 12:4–13 (KJV)

Likewise, teach the older women to be reverent in the way they live, not to be slanderers or addicted to much wine, but to teach what is good. Then they can train the younger women to love their husbands and children, to be self-controlled and pure, to be busy at home, to be kind, and to be subject to their husbands, so that no one will malign the word of God.

TITUS 2:3–5 (NIV)

Bid the older women similarly to be reverent and devout in their deportment as becomes those engaged in sacred service, not slanderers or slaves to drink. They are to give good counsel and be teachers of what is right and noble,

So that they will wisely train the young women to be sane and sober of mind (temperate, disciplined) and to love their husbands and their children,

To be self-controlled, chaste, homemakers, good-natured (kindhearted), adapting and subordinating themselves to their husbands, that the word of God may not be exposed to reproach (blasphemed or discredited).

Titus 2:3–5 (TAB)

The aged women likewise, that they be in behaviour as becometh holiness, not false accusers, not given to much wine, teachers of good things;

That they may teach the young women to be sober, to love their husbands, to love their children,

To be discreet, chaste, keepers at home, good, obedient to their own husbands, that the word of God be not blasphemed.

Titus 2:3–5 (KJV)

Again, it will be like a man going on a journey, which called his servants and entrusted his property to them. To one he gave five talents of money, to another two talents, and to another one talent, each according to his ability. Then he went on his journey. The man who had received the five talents went at once and put his money to work and gained five more. So also, the one with the two talents gained two more. But the man who had received the one talent went off, dug a hole in the ground and hid his master's money.

After a long time the master of those servants returned and settled accounts with them. The man who had received the five talents brought the other five. "Master," he said, "you entrusted me with five talents. See, I have gained five more."

His master replied, "Well done, good and faithful servant! You have been faithful with a few things; I will put you in charge of many things. Come and share your master's happiness!"

The man with the two talents also came. "Master," he said, "you entrusted me with two talents; see, I have gained two more."

His master replied, "Well done, good and faithful servant! You have been faithful with a few things; I will put you in charge of many things. Come and share your master's happiness!"

Then the man who had received the one talent came. "Master," he said, "I knew that you are a hard man, harvesting where you have not sown and gathering where you have not scattered seed. So I was afraid and went out and hid your talent in the ground. See, here is what belongs to you." His master replied, "you wicked, lazy servant! So you knew that I harvest where I have not sown and gather where I have not scattered seed? Well then, you should have put my money on deposit with the bankers, so that when I returned I would have received it back with interest. Take the talent from him and give it to the one who has the ten talents. For everyone who has will be given more, and he will have an abundance. Whoever does not have, even what he has will be taken from him. And throw that worthless servant outside, into the darkness, where there will be weeping and gnashing of teeth."

MATTHEW 25:14–30 (NIV)

For it is like a man who was about to take a

long journey, and he called his servants together and entrusted them with his property.

To one he gave five talents [probably about five thousand dollars], to another two, to another one— to each in proportion to his own personal ability. Then he departed and left the country.

He who had received the five talents went at once and traded with them, and he gained five talents more.

And likewise he who had received the two talents—he also gained two talents more.

But he who had received the one talent went and dug a hole in the ground and hid his master's money.

Now after a long time the master of those servants returned and settled accounts with them.

And he who had received the five talents came and brought him five more, saying, Master, you entrusted to me five talents; see, here I have gained five talents more.

His master said to him, well done, you upright (honorable, admirable) and faithful servant! You have been faithful and trustworthy over a little; I will put you in charge of much. Enter into and share the joy (the delight, the blessedness), which your master enjoys.

And he also who had the two talents came forward, saying, Master, you entrusted two talents to me; here I have gained two talents more.

His master said to him, well done, you upright (honorable, admirable) and faithful servant! You have been faithful and trustworthy over a little; I will put you in charge of much. Enter into and share the joy (the delight, the blessedness), which your master enjoys.

He who had received one talent also came forward, saying, Master, I knew you to be a harsh and hard man, reaping where you did not sow, and gathering where you had not winnowed [the grain].

So I was afraid, and I went and hid your talent in the ground. Here you have what is your own.

But his master answered him, you wicked and lazy and idle servant! Did you indeed know that I reap where I have not sowed and gather [grain] where I have not winnowed?

Then you should have invested my money with the bankers, and at my coming I would have received what was my own with interest.

So take the talent away from him and give it to the one who has the ten talents.

For to everyone who has will more be given, and he will be furnished richly so that he will have an abundance; but from the one who does not have, even what he does have will be taken away.

And throw the good-for-nothing servant into the outer darkness; there will be weeping and grinding of teeth.

MATTHEW 25:14–30 (TAB)

For the kingdom of heaven is as a man travelling into a far country, who called his own servants, and delivered unto them his goods.

And unto one he gave five talents, to another two, and to another one; to every man according to his several ability; and straightway took his journey.

Then he that had received the five talents went and traded with the same, and made them other five talents.

And likewise he that had received two, he also gained other two.

But he that had received one went and digged in the earth, and hid his Lord's money.

After a long time the Lord of those servants cometh, and reckoneth with them.

And so he that had received five talents came and brought other five talents, saying, Lord, thou deliveredst unto me five talents: behold, I have gained beside them five talents more.

His Lord said unto him, Well done, thou good and faithful servant: thou hast been faithful over a few things, I will make thee ruler over many things: enter thou into the joy of thy Lord.

He also that had received two talents came and said, Lord, thou deliveredst unto me two talents: behold, I have gained two other talents beside them.

His Lord said unto him, well done, good and faithful servant; thou hast been faithful over a few things, I will make thee ruler over many things: enter thou into the joy of thy Lord.

Then he which had received the one talent came and said, Lord, I knew thee that thou art an hard man, reaping where thou hast not sown, and gathering where thou hast not strawed:

And I was afraid, and went and hid thy talent in the earth: lo, there thou hast that is thine.

His Lord answered and said unto him, Thou wicked and slothful servant, thou knewest that I reap where I sowed not, and gather where I have not strawed:

Thou oughtest therefore to have put my money to the exchangers, and then at my coming I should have received mine own with usury.

Take therefore the talent from him, and give it unto him, which hath ten talents.

For unto every one that hath shall be given, and

he shall have abundance: but from him that hath not shall be taken away even that which he hath.

And cast ye the unprofitable servant into outer darkness: there shall be weeping and gnashing of teeth.

MATTHEW 25:14–30 (KJV)

I tell you the truth, unless a kernel of wheat falls to the ground and dies, it remains only a single seed. But if it dies, it produces many seeds. The man who loves his life will lose it, while the man who hates his life in this world will keep it for eternal life. Whoever serves me must follow me; and where I am, my servant also will be. My Father will honor the one who serves me.

JOHN 12:24–26 (NIV)

I assure you, most solemnly I tell you, unless a grain of wheat falls into the earth and dies, it remains [just one grain; it never becomes more but lives] by itself alone. But if it dies, it produces many others and yields a rich harvest.

Anyone who loves his life loses it, but anyone

who hates his life in this world will keep it to life eternal. [Whoever has no love for, no concern for, no regard for his life here on earth, but despises it, preserves his life forever and ever.]

If anyone serves me, he must continue to follow Me [to cleave steadfastly to Me, conform wholly to My example in living and, if need be, in dying] and wherever I am, there will my servant be also. If anyone serves me, the Father will honor him.

JOHN 12:24–26 (TAB)

Verily, verily, I say unto you, except a corn of wheat fall into the ground and die, it abideth alone: but if it die, it bringeth forth much fruit.

He that loveth his life shall lose it; and he that hateth his life in this world shall keep it unto life eternal.

If any man serve me, let him follow me; and where I am, there shall also my servant be: if any man serve me, him will my Father honour.

JOHN 12:24–26 (KJV)

Suppose one of you wants to build a tower.

Will he not first sit down and estimate the cost to see if he has enough money to complete it? For if he lays the foundation and is not able to finish it, everyone who sees it will ridicule him, saying, "this fellow began to build and was not able to finish." Or suppose a king is about to go to war against another king. Will he not first sit down and consider whether he is able with ten thousand men to oppose the one coming against him with twenty thousand? If he is not able, he will send a delegation while the other is still a long way off and will ask for terms of peace. In the same way, any of you who does not give up everything he has cannot be my disciple.

LUKE 14:28–33 (NIV)

For which of you, wishing to build a farm building, does not first sit down and calculate the cost [to see] whether he has sufficient means to finish it?

Otherwise, when he has laid the foundation and is unable to complete [the building], all who see it will begin to mock and jeer at him,

Saying, This man began to build and was not able (worth enough) to finish.

Or what king, going out to engage in conflict with another king, will not first sit down and consider and take counsel whether he is able with ten thousand [men] to meet him who comes against him with twenty thousand?

And if he cannot [do so], when the other king is still a great way off, he sends an envoy and asks the terms of peace.

So then, any of you who does not forsake (renounce, surrender claim to, give up, say good-bye to) all that he has cannot be My disciple.

LUKE 14:28–33 (TAB)

For which of you, intending to build a tower, sitteth not down first, and counteth the cost, whether he have sufficient to finish it?

Lest haply, after he hath laid the foundation, and is not able to finish it, all that behold it begin to mock him,

Saying, This man began to build, and was not able to finish.

Or what king, going to make war against another king, sitteth not down first, and consulteth whether he be able with ten thousand to meet him that cometh against him with twenty thousand?

Or else, while the other is yet a great way off, he sendeth an ambassage, and desireth conditions of peace.

So likewise, whosoever he be of you that forsaketh not all that he hath, he cannot be my disciple.

LUKE 14:28–33 (KJV)

When the Son of Man comes in his glory, and all the angels with him, he will sit on his throne in heavenly glory. All the nations will be gathered before him, and he will separate the people one from another as a shepherd separates the sheep from the goats. He will put the sheep on his right and the goats on his left.

Then the King will say to those on his right, "Come, you who are blessed by my Father; take your inheritance, the kingdom prepared for you since the creation of the world. For I was hungry and you gave me something to eat, I was thirsty and you gave me something to drink, I was a stranger and you invited me in, I needed clothes and you clothed me, I was sick and you looked after me, I was in prison and you came to visit me."

Then the righteous will answer him, "Lord, when did we see you hungry and feed you, or thirsty and give you something to drink? When did we see you a stranger and invite you in, or needing clothes and clothe you? When did we see you sick or in prison and go to visit you?"

The King will reply, "I tell you the truth, whatever you did for one of the least of these brothers of mine, you did for me."

Then he will say to those on his left, "Depart from me, you who are cursed, into the eternal fire prepared for the devil and his angels. For I was hungry and you gave me nothing to eat, I was thirsty and you gave me nothing to drink, I was a stranger and you did not invite me in, I needed clothes and you did not clothe me, I was sick and in prison and you did not look after me."

They also will answer, "Lord, when did we see you hungry or thirsty or a stranger or needing clothes or sick or in prison, and did not help you?"

He will reply, "I tell you the truth, whatever you did not do for one of the least of these, you did not do for me."

Then they will go away to eternal punishment, but the righteous to eternal life.

MATTHEW 25:31–46 (NIV)

When the Son of Man comes in His glory (His majesty and splendor), and all the holy angels with Him, then He will sit on the throne of His glory.

All nations will be gathered before Him, and He will separate them [the people] from one another as a shepherd separates his sheep from the goats;

And He will cause the sheep to stand at His right hand, but the goats at His left.

Then the King will say to those at His right hand, Come, you blessed of My Father [you favored of God and appointed to eternal salvation], inherit (receive as your own) the kingdom prepared for you from the foundation of the world.

For I was hungry and you gave Me food, I was thirsty and you gave Me something to drink, I was a stranger and you brought Me together with yourselves and welcomed and entertained and lodged Me,

I was naked and you clothed Me, I was sick and you visited Me with help and ministering care, I was in prison and you came to see Me.

Then the just and upright will answer Him, Lord, when did we see You hungry and gave You food, or thirsty and gave You something to drink?

And when did we see You a stranger and welcomed and entertained You, or naked and clothed You?

And when did we see You sick or in prison and came to visit You?

And the King will reply to them, Truly I tell you, in so far as you did it for one of the least [in the estimation of men] of these My brethren, you did it for Me.

Then He will say to those at His left hand, Begone from Me, you cursed, into the eternal fire prepared for the devil and his angels!

For I was hungry and you gave Me no food, I was thirsty and you gave Me nothing to drink,

I was a stranger and you did not welcome Me and entertain Me, I was naked and you did not clothe Me, I was sick and in prison and you did not visit Me with help and ministering care.

Then they also [in their turn] will answer, Lord, when did we see You hungry or thirsty or a stranger or naked or sick or in prison, and did not minister to You?

And He will reply to them, Solemnly I declare to you, in so far as you failed to do it for the least [in the estimation of men] of these, you failed to do it for Me.

Then they will go away into eternal punishment, but those who are just and upright and in right standing with God into eternal life.

MATTHEW 25:31–46 (TAB)

When the Son of man shall come in his glory, and all the holy angels with him, then shall he sit upon the throne of his glory:

And before him shall be gathered all nations: and he shall separate them one from another, as a shepherd divideth his sheep from the goats:

And he shall set the sheep on his right hand, but the goats on the left.

Then shall the King say unto them on his right hand, Come, ye blessed of my Father, inherit the kingdom prepared for you from the foundation of the world:

For I was an hungred, and ye gave me meat: I was thirsty, and ye gave me drink: I was a stranger, and ye took me in:

Naked, and ye clothed me: I was sick, and ye visited me: I was in prison, and ye came unto me.

Then shall the righteous answer him, saying, Lord, when saw we thee an hungred, and fed thee? or thirsty, and gave thee drink?

When saw we thee a stranger, and took thee in? or naked, and clothed thee?

Or when saw we thee sick, or in prison, and came unto thee?

And the King shall answer and say unto them, Verily I say unto you, Inasmuch as ye have done it unto one of the least of these my brethren, ye have done it unto me.

Then shall he say also unto them on the left hand, Depart from me, ye cursed, into everlasting fire, prepared for the devil and his angels:

For I was an hungred, and ye gave me no meat: I was thirsty, and ye gave me no drink:

I was a stranger, and ye took me not in: naked, and ye clothed me not: sick, and in prison, and ye visited me not.

Then shall they also answer him, saying, Lord, when saw we thee an hungred, or athirst, or a stranger, or naked, or sick, or in prison, and did not minister unto thee?

Then shall he answer them, saying, Verily I say unto you, Inasmuch as ye did it not to one of the least of these, ye did it not to me.

And these shall go away into everlasting punishment: but the righteous into life eternal.

MATTHEW 25:31–46 (KJV)

Whoever gives heed to instruction prospers, and blessed is he who trusts in the LORD.

Proverbs 16:20 (NIV)

He who deals wisely and heeds [God's] word and counsel shall find good, and whoever leans on, trusts in, and is confident in the Lord—happy, blessed, and fortunate is he.

PROVERBS 16:20 (TAB)

He that handleth a matter wisely shall find good: and whoso trusteth in the LORD, happy is he.

PROVERBS 16:20 (KJV)

Priscilla—Teacher Tent Maker

After this, Paul left Athens and went to Corinth. There he met a Jew named Aquila, a native of Pontus, who had recently come from Italy with his wife Priscilla, because Claudius had ordered all the Jews to leave Rome. Paul went to see them, and because he was a tentmaker as they were, he stayed and worked with them.

ACTS 18:1–3 (NIV)

After this [Paul] departed from Athens and went to Corinth.

There he met a Jew named Aquila, a native of Pontus, recently arrived from Italy with Priscilla his wife, due to the fact that Claudius had issued an edict that all the Jews were to leave Rome. And [Paul] went to see them,

And because he was of the same occupation, he stayed with them; and they worked [together], for they were tentmakers by trade.

ACTS 18:1–3 (TAB)

After these things Paul departed from Athens, and came to Corinth;

And found a certain Jew named Aquila, born in Pontus, lately come from Italy, with his wife Priscilla; (because that Claudius had commanded all Jews to depart from Rome) and came unto them.

And because he was of the same craft, he abode with them, and wrought: for by their occupation they were tentmakers.

ACTS 18:1–3 (KJV)

Paul stayed on in Corinth for some time. Then he left the brothers and sailed for Syria, accompanied by Priscilla and Aquila. Before he sailed, he had his hair cut off at Cenchrea because of a vow he had taken. They arrived at Ephesus, where Paul left Priscilla and Aquila.

ACTS 18:18, 19 (NIV)

Afterward Paul remained many days longer, and then told the brethren farewell and sailed for Syria; and he was accompanied by Priscilla and

Aquila. At Cenchreae he [Paul] cut his hair, for he had made a vow.

ACTS 18:18, 19 (TAB)

And Paul after this tarried there yet a good while, and then took his leave of the brethren, and sailed thence into Syria, and with him Priscilla and Aquila; having shorn his head in Cenchrea: for he had a vow.

ACTS 18:18, 19 (KJV)

Meanwhile a Jew named Apollos, a native of Alexandria, came to Ephesus. He was a learned man, with a thorough knowledge of the Scriptures. He had been instructed in the way of the Lord, and he spoke with great fervor and taught about Jesus accurately, though he knew only the baptism of John. He began to speak boldly in the synagogue. When Priscilla and Aquila heard him, they invited him to their home and explained to him the way of God more adequately.

ACTS 18:24–26 (NIV)

Meanwhile, there was a Jew named Apollos,

a native of Alexandria, who came to Ephesus. He was a cultured and eloquent man, well versed and mighty in the Scriptures.

He had been instructed in the way of the Lord, and burning with spiritual zeal, he spoke and taught diligently and accurately the things concerning Jesus, though he was acquainted only with the baptism of John.

He began to speak freely (fearlessly and boldly) in the synagogue; but when Priscilla and Aquila heard him, they took him with them and expounded to him the way of God more definitely and accurately.

ACTS 18:24–26 (TAB)

And a certain Jew named Apollos, born at Alexandria, an eloquent man, and mighty in the scriptures, came to Ephesus.

This man was instructed in the way of the Lord; and being fervent in the spirit, he spake and taught diligently the things of the Lord, knowing only the baptism of John.

And he began to speak boldly in the synagogue: whom when Aquila and Priscilla had heard, they took him unto them, and expounded unto him the way of God more perfectly.

ACTS 18:24–26 (KJV)

Greet Priscilla and Aquila, my fellow workers in Christ Jesus. They risked their lives for me. Not only I but also all the churches of the Gentiles are grateful to them.

ROMANS 16:3–4 (NIV)

Give my greetings to Priscilla and Aquila, my fellow workers in Christ Jesus,

Who risked their lives [endangering their very necks] for my life. To them not only I but also all the churches among the Gentiles give thanks.

ROMANS 16:3–4 (TAB)

Greet Priscilla and Aquila my helpers in Christ Jesus:

Who have for my life laid down their own necks: unto whom not only I give thanks, but also all the churches of the Gentiles.

ROMANS 16:3–4 (KJV)

Lydia

Business Woman, Community Leader

On the Sabbath we went outside the city gate

to the river, where we expected to find a place of prayer. We sat down and began to speak to the women who had gathered there. One of those listening was a woman named Lydia, a dealer in purple cloth from the city of Thyatira, who was a worshiper of God. The Lord opened her heart to respond to Paul's message. When she and the members of her household were baptized, she invited us to her home. "If you consider me a believer in the Lord," she said, "come and stay at my house." And she persuaded us.

ACTS 16:13–15 (NIV)

And on the Sabbath day we went outside the [city's] gate to the bank of the river where we supposed there was an [accustomed] place of prayer, and we sat down and addressed the women who had assembled there.

One of those who listened to us was a woman named Lydia, from the city of Thyatira, a dealer in fabrics dyed in purple. She was [already] a worshiper of God, and the Lord opened her heart to pay attention to what was said by Paul.

And when she was baptized along with her household, she earnestly entreated us, saying, If in your opinion I am one really convinced [that Jesus is the Messiah and the Author of salvation] and that I will be faithful to the Lord, come to my house and stay. And she induced us [to do it].

ACTS 16:13–15 (TAB)

And on the Sabbath we went out of the city by a river side, where prayer was wont to be made; and we sat down, and spake unto the women which resorted thither.

And a certain woman named Lydia, a seller of purple, of the city of Thyatira, which worshipped God, heard us: whose heart the Lord opened, that she attended unto the things which were spoken of Paul.

And when she was baptized, and her household, she besought us, saying, If ye have judged me to be faithful to the Lord, come into my house, and abide there. And she constrained us.

ACTS 16:13–15 (KJV)

Rahab

Grace under Fire

Then Joshua son of Nun secretly sent two spies from Shittim. "Go, look over the land," he said, "especially Jericho." So they went and entered the house of a prostitute named Rahab and stayed there.

(But she had taken them up to the roof and

hidden them under the stalks of flax she had laid out on the roof.) So the men set out in pursuit of the spies on the road that leads to the fords of the Jordan, and as soon as the pursuers had gone out, the gate was shut.

Before the spies lay down for the night, she went up on the roof and said to them, "I know that the LORD has given this land to you and that a great fear of you has fallen on us, so that all who live in this country are melting in fear because of you ... . Now then, please swear to me by the LORD that you will show kindness to my family, because I have shown kindness to you. Give me a sure sign that you will spare the lives of my father and mother, my brothers and sisters, and all who belong to them, and that you will save us from death."

"Our lives for your lives!" the men assured her. "If you don't tell what we are doing, we will treat you kindly and faithfully when the LORD gives us the land."

JOSHUA 2:1, 6–9, 12–14 (NIV)

Joshua Son of Nun sent two men secretly from Shittim as scouts, saying, Go, view the land, especially Jericho. And they went and came to the house of a harlot named Rahab and lodged there. But she had brought them up to the roof and hidden them under the stalks of flax which she had laid in order there. So the men pursued them to the Jordan as far as the fords. As soon as the pursuers had gone, the city's gate was shut. Before the two men had lain down, Rahab came up to them on the roof, And she said to the men, I know that the Lord has given you the land and that your terror is fallen upon us and that all the inhabitants of the land faint because of you ... Now then, I pray you, swear to me by the Lord, since I have shown you kindness, that you also will show kindness to my father's house, and give me a sure sign, And save alive my father and mother, my brothers and sisters, and all they have, and deliver us from death.

And the men said to her, Our lives for yours! If you do not tell this business of ours, then when the Lord gives us the land we will deal kindly and faithfully with you.

JOSHUA 2:1, 6–9, 12–14 (TAB)

And Joshua the son of Nun sent out of Shittim two men to spy secretly, saying, Go view the land, even Jericho. And they went, and came into an harlot's house, named Rahab, and lodged there. But she had brought them up to the roof of the house, and hid them with the stalks of flax, which she had laid in order upon the roof. And the men pursued after them the way to Jordan unto the fords: and as soon as they which pursued after them were gone out, they shut the gate. And before they were laid down, she came up unto them upon the roof;

And she said unto the men, I know that the LORD hath given you the land, and that your terror is fallen upon us, and that all the inhabitants of the land faint because of you ...

Now therefore, I pray you, swear unto me by the LORD, since I have shewed you kindness, that ye will also shew kindness unto my father's house, and give me a true token: And that ye will save alive my father, and my mother, and my brethren, and my sisters, and all that they have, and deliver our lives from death.

And the men answered her, our life for yours, if ye utter not this our business. And it shall be, when the LORD hath given us the land, that we will deal kindly and truly with thee.

JOSHUA 2:1, 6–9, 12–14 (KJV)

The city and all that is in it are to be devoted to the LORD. Only Rahab the prostitute and all who are with her in her house shall be spared, because she hid the spies we sent ... Joshua said to the two men who had spied out the land, "Go into the prostitute's house and bring her out and all who belong to her, in accordance with your oath to her." So the young men who had done the spying went in and brought out Rahab, her father and mother and brothers and all who belonged to her. They brought out her entire family and put them in a place outside the camp of Israel.

Then they burned the whole city and everything in it, but they put the silver and gold and the articles of bronze and iron into the treasury of the Lord's house. But Joshua spared Rahab the prostitute, with her family and all who belonged to her, because she hid the men Joshua had sent as spies to Jericho—and she lives among the Israelites to this day.

JOSHUA 6:17, 22–25 (NIV)

And the city and all that is in it shall be devoted to the Lord [for destruction]; only Rahab the harlot and all who are with her in her house shall live, because she hid the messengers whom we sent... But Joshua said to the two men who had spied out the land, Go into the harlot's house and bring out the woman and all she has, as you swore to her. So the young men, the spies, went in and brought out Rahab, her father and mother, her brethren, and all that she had; and they brought out all her kindred and set them outside the camp of Israel. And they burned the city with fire and all that was in it; only the silver, the gold, and the vessels of bronze and of iron they put into the treasury of the house of the Lord. So Joshua saved Rahab the harlot, with her father's household and all that she had; and she lives in Israel even to this day, because she hid the messengers whom Joshua sent to spy out Jericho.

JOSHUA 6:17, 22–25 (TAB)

And the city shall be accursed, even it, and all that are therein, to the LORD: only Rahab the harlot shall live, she and all that are with her in the house, because she hid the messengers that we sent... But Joshua had said unto the two men that had spied out the country, Go into the harlot's house, and bring out thence the woman, and all that she hath, as ye sware unto her. And the young men that were spies went in, and brought out Rahab, and her father, and her mother, and her brethren, and all that she had; and they brought out all her kindred, and left them without the camp of Israel. And they burnt the city with fire, and all that was therein: only the silver, and the gold, and the vessels of brass and of iron, they put into the treasury of the house of the LORD. And Joshua saved Rahab the harlot alive, and her father's household, and all that she had; and she dwelleth in Israel even unto this day;

because she hid the messengers, which Joshua sent to spy out Jericho.

JOSHUA 6:17, 22–25 (KJV)

Salmon the father of Boaz, whose mother was Rahab, Boaz the father of Obed, whose mother was Ruth, Obed the father of Jesse...

MATTHEW 1:5 (NIV, AUTHOR'S EMPHASIS)

Salmon the father of Boaz, whose mother was Rahab, Boaz the father of Obed, whose mother was Ruth, Obed the father of Jesse...

MATTHEW 1:5 (TAB, AUTHOR'S EMPHASIS)

And Salmon begat Booz of Rachab; and Booz begat Obed of Ruth; and Obed begat Jesse...

MATTHEW 1:5 (KJV, AUTHOR'S EMPHASIS)

By faith the prostitute Rahab, because she welcomed the spies, was not killed with those who were disobedient.

HEBREWS: 11:31 (NIV)

[Prompted] by faith Rahab the prostitute was not destroyed along with those who refused to believe and obey, because she had received the spies in peace [without enmity] ...

HEBREWS: 11:31 (TAB)

By faith the harlot Rahab perished not with them that believed not, when she had received the spies with peace.

HEBREWS: 11:31 (KJV)

In the same way, was not even Rahab the prostitute considered righteous for what she did when she gave lodging to the spies and sent them off in a different direction?

JAMES 2:25 (NIV)

So also with Rahab the harlot—was she not shown to be justified (pronounced righteous before

God) by [good] deeds when she took in the scouts (spies) and sent them away by a different route?

JAMES 2:25 (TAB)

Likewise also was not Rahab the harlot justified by works, when she had received the messengers, and had sent them out another way?

JAMES 2:25 (KJV)

Esther

Taking a Stand

Mordecai had a cousin named Hadassah, whom he had brought up because she had neither father nor mother. This girl, who was also known as Esther, was lovely in form and features, and Mordecai had taken her as his own daughter when her father and mother died.

When the king's order and edict had been proclaimed, many girls were brought to the citadel of Susa and put under the care of Hegai. Esther also was taken to the king's palace and entrusted to Hegai, who had charge of the harem. The girl pleased him and won his favor. Immediately he provided her with her beauty treatments and special food. He assigned to her seven maids selected from the king's palace and moved her and her maids into the best place in the harem. Esther had not revealed her nationality and family background, because Mordecai had forbidden her to do so.

When the turn came for Esther (the girl Mordecai had adopted, the daughter of his uncle Abihail) to go to the king, she asked for nothing other than what Hegai, the king's eunuch who was in charge of the harem, suggested. And Esther won the favor of everyone who saw her.

Now the king was attracted to Esther more than to any of the other women, and she won his favor and approval more than any of the other virgins. So he set a royal crown on her head and made her queen instead of Vashti.

BOOK OF ESTHER 2:7–10, 15, 17 (NIV)

He had brought up Hadassah, that is Esther, his uncle's daughter, for she had neither father nor mother. The maiden was beautiful and lovely, and when her father and mother died, Mordecai took her as his own daughter.

So when the king's command and his decree were proclaimed and when many maidens were gathered in Shushan the capital under the custody of Hegai, Esther also was taken to the king's house into the custody of Hegai, keeper of the women.

And the maiden pleased [Hegai] and obtained his favor. And he speedily gave her the things for her purification and her portion of food and the seven chosen maids to be given her from the king's palace; and he removed her and her maids to the best [apartment] in the harem.

Esther had not made known her nationality or her kindred, for Mordecai had charged her not to do so.

Now when the turn for Esther the daughter of Abihail, the uncle of Mordecai who had taken her as his own daughter, had come to go in to the king, she required nothing but what Hegai the king's attendant, the keeper of the women, suggested. And Esther won favor in the sight of all who saw her.

And the king loved Esther more than all the women, and she obtained grace and favor in his sight more than all the maidens, so that he set the royal crown on her head and made her queen instead of Vashti.

BOOK OF ESTHER 2:7–10, 15, 17 (TAB)

And he brought up Hadassah, that is, Esther, his uncle's daughter: for she had neither father nor mother, and the maid was fair and beautiful; whom Mordecai, when her father and mother were dead, took for his own daughter.

So it came to pass, when the king's commandment and his decree was heard, and when many maidens were gathered together unto Shushan the palace, to the custody of Hegai, that Esther was brought also unto the king's house, to the custody of Hegai, keeper of the women.

And the maiden pleased him, and she obtained kindness of him; and he speedily gave her things for purification, with such things as belonged to her, and seven maidens, which were meet to be given her, out of the king's house: and he preferred her and her maids unto the best place of the house of the women.

Esther had not shewed her people nor her kindred: for Mordecai had charged her that she should not shew it.

Now when the turn of Esther, the daughter of Abihail the uncle of Mordecai, who had taken her for his daughter, was come to go in unto the king, she required nothing but what Hegai the king's chamberlain, the keeper of the women, appointed. And Esther obtained favour in the sight of all them that looked upon her.

And the king loved Esther above all the women, and she obtained grace and favour in his sight more than all the virgins; so that he set the royal crown upon her head, and made her queen instead of Vashti.

BOOK OF ESTHER 2:7–10, 15, 17 (KJV)

Then she instructed him to say to Mordecai, "All the king's officials and the people of the royal provinces know that for any man or woman who approaches the king in the inner court without being summoned the king has but one law: that he be put to death. The only exception to this is for the king to extend the gold scepter to him and spare his life. But thirty days have passed since I was called to go to the king."

When Esther's words were reported to Mordecai, he sent back this answer: "Do not think that because you are in the king's house you alone of all the Jews will escape. For if you remain silent at this time, relief and deliverance for the Jews will arise from another place, but you and your father's family will perish. And who knows but that you have come to royal position for such a time as this?"

Then Esther sent this reply to Mordecai: "Go, gather together all the Jews who are in Susa, and fast for me. Do not eat or drink for three days, night or day. I and my maids will fast as you do. When this is done, I will go to the king, even though it is against the law. And if I perish, I perish."

BOOK OF ESTHER 4:10–16 (NIV)

Then Esther spoke to Hathach and gave him a message for Mordecai, saying,

All the king's servants and the people of the king's provinces know that any person, be it man or woman, who shall go into the inner court to the king without being called shall be put to death; there is but one law for him, except [him] to whom the king shall hold out the golden scepter, that he may live. But I have not been called to come to the king for these thirty days. And they told Mordecai what Esther said.

Then Mordecai told them to return this answer to Esther, Do not flatter yourself that you shall escape in the king's palace any more than all the other Jews.

For if you keep silent at this time, relief and deliverance shall arise for the Jews from elsewhere, but you and your father's house will perish. And who knows but that you have come to the kingdom for such a time as this and for this very occasion?

Then Esther told them to give this answer to Mordecai, Go, gather together all the Jews that are present in Shushan, and fast for me; and neither eat nor drink for three days, night or day. I also and my maids will fast as you do. Then I will go to the king, though it is against the law; and if I perish, I perish.

BOOK OF ESTHER 4:10–16 (TAB)

Again Esther spake unto Hatach, and gave him commandment unto Mordecai; All the king's servants, and the people of the king's provinces, do know, that whosoever, whether man or women, shall come unto the king into the inner court, who is not called, there is one law of his to put him to death, except such to whom the king shall hold out the golden sceptre, that he may live: but I have not been called to come in unto the king these thirty days.

And they told to Mordecai Esther's words.

Then Mordecai commanded to answer Esther, Think not with thyself that thou shalt escape in the king's house, more than all the Jews.

For if thou altogether holdest thy peace at this time, then shall there enlargement and deliverance arise to the Jews from another place; but thou and thy father's house shall be destroyed: and who knoweth whether thou art come to the kingdom for such a time as this?

Then Esther bade them return Mordecai this answer,

Go, gather together all the Jews that are present in Shushan, and fast ye for me, and neither eat nor drink three days, night or day: I also and my maidens will fast likewise; and so will I go in unto the king, which is not according to the law: and if I perish, I perish.

BOOK OF ESTHER 4:10–16 (KJV)

So the king and Haman went to dine with Queen Esther, and as they were drinking wine on that second day, the king again asked, "Queen Esther, what is your petition? It will be given you. What is your request? Even up to half the kingdom, it will be granted."

Then Queen Esther answered, "If I have found favor with you, O king, and if it pleases your majesty, grant me my life—this is my petition. And spare my people—this is my request.

BOOK OF ESTHER 7:1–3 (NIV)

So the king and Haman came to dine with Esther the queen.

And the king said again to Esther on the second day when wine was being served, what is your petition, Queen Esther? It shall be granted. And what is your request? Even to the half of the kingdom, it shall be performed.

Then Queen Esther said, if I have found favor in your sight, O king and if it pleases the king, let my life be given me at my petition and my people at my request.

BOOK OF ESTHER 7:1–3 (TAB)

So the king and Haman came to banquet with Esther the queen.

And the king said again unto Esther on the second day at the banquet of wine, what is thy petition, queen Esther? And it shall be granted thee: and what is thy request? And it shall be performed, even to the half of the kingdom.

Then Esther the queen answered and said, if I have found favour in thy sight, O king, and if it pleases the king, let my life be given me at my petition, and my people at my request.

BOOK OF ESTHER 7:1–3 (KJV)

Deborah

Warrior Wife

Deborah, a prophetess, the wife of Lappidoth, was leading Israel at that time. She held court under the Palm of Deborah between Ramah and Bethel in the hill country of Ephraim, and the Israelites came to her to have their disputes decided. She sent for Barak son of Abinoam from Kedesh in Naphtali and said to him, "The LORD, the God of Israel, commands you: 'Go, take with you ten thousand men of Naphtali and

Zebulun and lead the way to Mount Tabor. I will lure Sisera, the commander of Jabin's army, with his chariots and his troops to the Kishon River and give him into your hands.'"

Barak said to her, "If you go with me, I will go; but if you don't go with me, I won't go."

"Very well," Deborah said, "I will go with you. But because of the way you are going about this, the honor will not be yours, for the LORD will hand Sisera over to a woman." So Deborah went with Barak to Kedesh,

Then Deborah said to Barak, "Go! This is the day the LORD has given Sisera into your hands. Has not the LORD gone ahead of you?" So Barak went down Mount Tabor, followed by ten thousand men.

JUDGES 4:4–9, 14 (NIV)

Now Deborah, a prophetess, the wife of Lappidoth, judged Israel at that time. She sat under the palm tree of Deborah between Ramah and Bethel in the hill country of Ephraim, and the Israelites came up to her for judgment.

And she sent and called Barak son of Abinoam from Kedesh in Naphtali and said to him, Has not the Lord, the God of Israel, commanded [you], Go, gather your men at Mount Tabor, taking ten thousand men from the tribes of Naphtali and Zebulun?

And I will draw out Sisera, the general of Jabin's army, to meet you at the river Kishon with his chariots and his multitude, and I will deliver him into your hand?

And Barak said to her, If you will go with me, then I will go; but if you will not go with me, I will not go.

And she said, I will surely go with you; nevertheless, the trip you take will not be for your glory, for the Lord will sell Sisera into the hand of a woman. And Deborah arose and went with Barak to Kedesh.

And Deborah said to Barak, Up! For this is the day when the Lord has given Sisera into your hand. Is not the Lord gone out before you? So Barak went down from Mount Tabor with ten thousand men following him.

JUDGES 4:4–9, 14 (TAB)

And Deborah, a prophetess, the wife of Lapidoth, she judged Israel at that time. And she dwelt under the palm tree of Deborah between Ramah and Bethel in mount Ephraim: and the children of Israel came up to her for judgment.

And she sent and called Barak the son of Abinoam out of Kedeshnaphtali, and said unto him, Hath not the LORD God of Israel commanded, saying, Go and draw toward mount Tabor, and take with thee ten thousand men of the children of Naphtali and of the children of Zebulun?

And I will draw unto thee to the river Kishon Sisera, the captain of Jabin's army, with his chariots and his multitude; and I will deliver him into thine hand.

And Barak said unto her, if thou wilt go with me, then I will go: but if thou wilt not go with me, then I will not go.

And she said, I will surely go with thee: notwithstanding the journey that thou takest shall not be for thine honour; for the LORD shall sell Sisera into the hand of a woman. And Deborah arose, and went with Barak to Kedesh

And Deborah said unto Barak, up; for this is the day in which the LORD hath delivered Sisera into thine hand: is not the LORD gone out before thee? So Barak went down from mount Tabor, and ten thousand men after him.

JUDGES 4:4–9, 14 (KJV)

Tamar

Overcomer

Judah got a wife for Er, his firstborn, and her name was Tamar. But Er, Judah's firstborn, was wicked in the Lord's sight; so the LORD put him to death.

Then Judah said to Onan, "Lie with your brother's wife and fulfill your duty to her as a brother-in-law to produce offspring for your brother." But Onan knew that the offspring would not be his; so whenever he lay with his brother's wife, he spilled his semen on the ground to keep from producing offspring for his brother. What he did was wicked in the Lord's sight; so he put him to death also. Judah then said to his daughter-in-law Tamar, "Live as a widow in your father's house until my son Shelah grows up." For he thought, "He may die too, just like his brothers." So Tamar went to live in her father's house.

After a long time Judah's wife, the daughter of Shua, died. When Judah had recovered from his grief, he went up to Timnah, to the men who were shearing his sheep, and his friend Hirah the Adullamite went with him.

When Tamar was told, "Your father-in-law is on his way to Timnah to shear his sheep," she took off her widow's clothes, covered herself with a veil to disguise herself, and then sat down at the entrance to Enaim, which is on the road to Timnah. For she saw that, though Shelah had now grown up, she had not been given to him as his wife.

When Judah saw her, he thought she was a prostitute, for she had covered her face.

GENESIS 38:6–15 (NIV)

Now Judah took a wife for Er, his firstborn; her name was Tamar. And Er, Judah's firstborn, was wicked in the sight of the Lord, and the Lord slew him. Then Judah told Onan, Marry your brother's widow; live with her and raise offspring for your brother. But Onan knew that the family would not be his, so when he cohabited with his brother's widow, he prevented conception, lest he should raise up a child for his brother. And the thing which he did displeased the Lord; therefore He slew him also. Then Judah said to Tamar, his daughter-in-law, Remain a widow at your father's house till Shelah my [youngest] son is grown; for he thought, Lest perhaps [if Shelah should marry her] he would die also, as his brothers did. So Tamar went and lived in her father's house. But later Judah's wife, the daughter of Shuah, died; and when Judah was comforted, he went up to his sheepshearers at Timnath with his friend Hirah the Adullamite. Then it was told Tamar, Listen, your father-in-law is going up to Timnath to shear his sheep. So she put off her widow's garments and covered herself with a veil, wrapped herself up [in disguise], and sat in the entrance of Enaim, which is by the road to Timnath; for she saw that Shelah was grown and she was not given to him as his wife. When Judah saw

her, he thought she was a harlot or devoted prostitute [under a vow to her goddess], for she had
covered her face [as such women did].

Genesis 38:6–15 (TAB)

And Judah took a wife for Er his firstborn,
whose name was Tamar.

And Er, Judah's firstborn, was wicked in the
sight of the LORD; and the LORD slew him.

And Judah said unto Onan, Go in unto thy
brother's wife, and marry her, and raise up seed to
thy brother.

And Onan knew that the seed should not be
his; and it came to pass, when he went in unto his
brother's wife, that he spilled it on the ground, lest
that he should give seed to his brother.

And the thing, which he did, displeased the
LORD: wherefore he slew him also.

Then said Judah to Tamar his daughter in law,
Remain a widow at thy father's house, till Shelah
my son be grown: for he said, Lest peradventure he
die also, as his brethren did. And Tamar went and
dwelt in her father's house.

And in process of time the daughter of Shuah
Judah's wife died; and Judah was comforted, and
went up unto his sheepshearers to Timnath, he and
his friend Hirah the Adullamite.

And it was told Tamar, saying, Behold thy father in law goeth up to Timnath to shear his sheep.

And she put her widow's garments off from her, and covered her with a vail, and wrapped herself, and sat in an open place, which is by the way to Timnath; for she saw that Shelah was grown, and she was not given unto him to wife.

When Judah saw her, he thought her to be an harlot; because she had covered her face.

GENESIS 38:6–15 (KJV)

About three months later Judah was told, "Your daughter-in-law Tamar is guilty of prostitution, and as a result she is now pregnant."

Judah said, "Bring her out and have her burned to death!" As she was being brought out, she sent a message to her father-in-law. "I am pregnant by the man who owns these," she said. And she added, "See if you recognize whose seal and cord and staff these are."

Judah recognized them and said, "She is more righteous than I, since I wouldn't give her to my son Shelah." And he did not sleep with her again.

GENESIS 38:24–26 (NIV)

But about three months later Judah was told, Tamar your daughter-in-law has played the harlot, and also she is with child by her lewdness. And Judah said, Bring her forth and let her be burned!

When she was brought forth, she [took the things he had given her in pledge and] sent [them] to her father-in-law, saying, I am with child by the man to whom these articles belong. Then she added, Make out clearly, I pray you, to whom these belong, the signet [seal], [signet] cord, and staff.

And Judah acknowledged them and said; She has been more righteous and just than I, because I did not give her to Shelah my son. And he did not cohabit with her again.

GENESIS 38:24–26 (TAB)

And it came to pass about three months after, that it was told Judah, saying, Tamar thy daughter in law hath played the harlot; and also, behold, she is with child by whoredom. And Judah said, bring her forth, and let her be burnt.

When she was brought forth, she sent to her father in law, saying, By the man, whose these are, am I with child: and she said, Discern, I pray thee, whose are these, the signet, and bracelets, and staff.

And Judah acknowledged them, and said, She

hath been more righteous than I; because that I gave her not to Shelah my son. And he knew her again no more.

GENESIS 38:24–26 (KJV)

Judah the father of Perez and Zerah, whose mother was Tamar, Perez the father of Hezron, Hezron the father of Ram...

MATTHEW 1:3 (NIV, AUTHOR'S EMPHASIS)

Judah the father of Perez and Zerah, whose mother was Tamar, Perez the father of Hezron, Hezron the father of Aram...

MATTHEW 1:3 (TAB, AUTHOR'S EMPHASIS)

And Judas begat Phares and Zara of Thamar; and Phares begat Esrom; and Esrom begat Aram...

MATTHEW 1:3 (KJV, AUTHOR'S EMPHASIS)

Ruth

Faithful Outcast

Return home, my daughters; I am too old to have another husband. Even if I thought there was

161

still hope for me—even if I had a husband tonight and then gave birth to sons—would you wait until they grew up? Would you remain unmarried for them? No, my daughters. It is more bitter for me than for you, because the Lord's hand has gone out against me!

At this they wept again. Then Orpah kissed her mother-in-law good-bye, but Ruth clung to her.

"Look," said Naomi, "your sister-in-law is going back to her people and her gods. Go back with her."

But Ruth replied, "Don't urge me to leave you or to turn back from you. Where you go I will go, and where you stay I will stay. Your people will be my people and your God my God. Where you die I will die, and there I will be buried. May the LORD deal with me, be it ever so severely, if anything but death separates you and me." When Naomi realized that Ruth was determined to go with her, she stopped urging her.

BOOK OF RUTH 1:12–18 (NIV)

Turn back, my daughters, go; for I am too old to have a husband. If I should say I have hope, even if I should have a husband tonight and should bear sons,

Would you therefore wait till they were grown? Would you therefore refrain from marrying? No, my daughters; it is far more bitter for me than for you that the hand of the Lord is gone out against me.

Then they wept aloud again; and Orpah kissed her mother-in-law [good-bye], but Ruth clung to her.

And Naomi said, See, your sister-in-law has gone back to her people and to her gods; return after your sister-in-law.

And Ruth said, Urge me not to leave you or to turn back from following you; for where you go I will go, and where you lodge I will lodge. Your people shall be my people and your God my God.

Where you die I will die, and there will I be buried. The Lord do so to me, and more also, if anything but death parts me from you.

When Naomi saw that Ruth was determined to go with her, she said no more.

BOOK OF RUTH 1:12–18 (TAB)

Turn again, my daughters, go your way; for I am too old to have an husband. If I should say, I have hope, if I should have an husband also to night, and should also bear sons;

Would ye tarry for them till they were grown? Would ye stay for them from having husbands? nay, my daughters; for it grieveth me much for your sakes that the hand of the LORD is gone out against me.

And they lifted up their voice, and wept again:

and Orpah kissed her mother-in-law; but Ruth clave unto her.

And she said, Behold, thy sister-in-law is gone back unto her people, and unto her gods: return thou after thy sister-in-law.

And Ruth said, Intreat me not to leave thee, or to return from following after thee: for whither thou goest, I will go; and where thou lodgest, I will lodge: thy people shall be my people, and thy God my God:

Where thou diest, will I die, and there will I be buried: the LORD do so to me, and more also, if ought but death part thee and me.

When she saw that she was stedfastly minded to go with her, then she left speaking unto her.

BOOK OF RUTH 1:12–18 (KJV)

Just then Boaz arrived from Bethlehem and greeted the harvesters, "The LORD be with you!" "The LORD bless you!" they called back.

Boaz asked the foreman of his harvesters, "Whose young woman is that?"

The foreman replied, "She is the Moabitess who came back from Moab with Naomi. She said, 'Please let me glean and gather among the sheaves behind the harvesters.' She went into the field and has worked steadily from morning till now, except for a short rest in the shelter."

So Boaz said to Ruth, "My daughter, listen to me. Don't go and glean in another field and don't go away from here. Stay here with my servant girls. Watch the field where the men are harvesting, and follow along after the girls. I have told the men not to touch you. And whenever you are thirsty, go and get a drink from the water jars the men have filled."

At this, she bowed down with her face to the ground. She exclaimed, "Why have I found such favor in your eyes that you notice me—a foreigner?"

Boaz replied, "I've been told all about what you have done for your mother-in-law since the death of your husband—how you left your father and mother and your homeland and came to live with a people you did not know before. May the LORD repay you for what you have done. May you be richly rewarded by the LORD, the God of Israel, under whose wings you have come to take refuge."

"May I continue to find favor in your eyes, my

Lord," she said. "You have given me comfort and have spoken kindly to your servant—though I do not have the standing of one of your servant girls."

Book of Ruth 2:4–13 (NIV)

And behold, Boaz came from Bethlehem and said to the reapers, The Lord be with you! And they answered him, The Lord bless you!

Then Boaz said to his servant who was set over the reapers, whose maiden is this?

And the servant set over the reapers answered, She is the Moabitish girl who came back with Naomi from the country of Moab.

And she said, I pray you, let me glean and gather after the reapers among the sheaves. So she came and has continued from early morning until now, except when she rested a little in the house.

Then Boaz said to Ruth, Listen, my daughter, do not go to glean in another field or leave this one, but stay here close by my maidens.

Watch which field they reap, and follow them. Have I not charged the young men not to molest you? And when you are thirsty, go to the vessels and drink what the young men have drawn.

Then she fell on her face, bowing to the ground, and said to him, why have I found favor in your eyes that you should notice me, when I am a foreigner?

And Boaz said to her, I have been made fully aware of all you have done for your mother-in-law since the death of your husband, and how you have left your father and mother and the land of your birth and have come to a people unknown to you before.

The Lord recompense you for what you have done, and a full reward be given you by the Lord, the God of Israel, under Whose wings you have come to take refuge!

Then she said, let me find favor in your sight, my Lord. For you have comforted me and have spoken to the heart of your maidservant, though I am not as one of your maidservants.

BOOK OF RUTH 2:4–13 (TAB)

And, behold, Boaz came from Bethlehem, and said unto the reapers, The LORD be with you. And they answered him, The LORD bless thee.

Then said Boaz unto his servant that was set over the reapers, whose damsel is this?

And the servant that was set over the reapers answered and said, It is the Moabitish damsel that came back with Naomi out of the country of Moab:

And she said, I pray you, let me glean and gather after the reapers among the sheaves: so she came, and hath continued even from the morning until now, that she tarried a little in the house.

Then said Boaz unto Ruth, Hearest thou not, my daughter? Go not to glean in another field, neither go from hence, but abide here fast by my maidens:

Let thine eyes be on the field that they do reap, and go thou after them: have I not charged the young men that they shall not touch thee? and when thou art athirst, go unto the vessels, and drink of that which the young men have drawn.

Then she fell on her face, and bowed herself to the ground, and said unto him, Why have I found grace in thine eyes, that thou shouldest take knowledge of me, seeing I am a stranger?

And Boaz answered and said unto her, It hath fully been shewed me, all that thou hast done unto thy mother in law since the death of thine husband: and how thou hast left thy father and thy mother, and the land of thy nativity, and art come unto a people which thou knewest not heretofore.

The LORD recompense thy work, and a full reward be given thee of the LORD God of Israel, under whose wings thou art come to trust.

Then she said, Let me find favour in thy sight, my Lord; for that thou hast comforted me, and for that thou hast spoken friendly unto thine handmaid, though I be not like unto one of thine hand-maidens.

BOOK OF RUTH 2:4–13 (KJV)

⌁

So Boaz took Ruth and she became his wife. Then he went to her, and the LORD enabled her to conceive, and she gave birth to a son. The women said to Naomi: "Praise be to the LORD, who this day has not left you without a kinsman-redeemer. May he become famous throughout Israel! He will renew your life and sustain you in your old age. For your daughter-in-law, who loves you and who is better to you than seven sons, has given him birth."

Then Naomi took the child, laid him in her lap and cared for him. The women living there said, "Naomi has a son." And they named him Obed. He was the father of Jesse, the father of David.

BOOK OF RUTH 4:13–17 (NIV)

So Boaz took Ruth and she became his wife. And he went in to her, and the Lord caused her to conceive, and she bore a son.

And the women said to Naomi, Blessed be the

Lord, Who has not left you this day without a close kinsman, and may his name be famous in Israel.

And may he be to you a restorer of life and a nourisher and supporter in your old age, for your daughter-in-law who loves you, who is better to you than seven sons, has borne him.

Then Naomi took the child and laid him in her bosom and became his nurse.

And her neighbor women gave him a name, saying, A son is born to Naomi. They named him Obed. He was the father of Jesse, the father of David [the ancestor of Jesus Christ].

BOOK OF RUTH 4:13–17 (TAB)

So Boaz took Ruth, and she was his wife: and when he went in unto her, the LORD gave her conception, and she bare a son.

And the women said unto Naomi, Blessed be the LORD, which hath not left thee this day without a kinsman, that his name may be famous in Israel.

And he shall be unto thee a restorer of thy life, and a nourisher of thine old age: for thy daughter in law, which loveth thee, which is better to thee than seven sons, hath born him.

And Naomi took the child, and laid it in her bosom, and became nurse unto it.

And the women her neighbours gave it a name, saying, there is a son born to Naomi; and they called his name Obed: he is the father of Jesse, the father of David.

BOOK OF RUTH 4:13–17 (KJV)

Naomi

A Change of Heart

Now Elimelech, Naomi's husband, died, and she was left with her two sons. They married Moabite women, one named Orpah and the other Ruth. After they had lived there about ten years, both Mahlon and Kilion also died, and Naomi was left without her two sons and her husband.

BOOK OF RUTH 1:3–5 (NIV)

But Elimelech, who Naomi's husband, died, and she was left with her two sons.

And they took wives of the women of Moab; the name of the one was Orpah and the name of the other Ruth. They dwelt there about ten years;

And Mahlon and Chilion died also, both of them, so the woman was bereft of her two sons and her husband.

BOOK OF RUTH 1:3–5 (TAB)

And Elimelech Naomi's husband died; and she was left, and her two sons.

And they took them wives of the women of Moab; the name of the one was Orpah, and the

171

name of the other Ruth: and they dwelled there about ten years.

And Mahlon and Chilion died also both of them; and the woman was left of her two sons and her husband.

BOOK OF RUTH 1:3–5 (KJV)

So the two women went on until they came to Bethlehem. When they arrived in Bethlehem, the whole town was stirred because of them, and the women exclaimed, "Can this be Naomi?" "Don't call me Naomi," she told them. "Call me Mara, because the Almighty has made my life very bitter. I went away full, but the LORD has brought me back empty. Why call me Naomi? The LORD has afflicted me; the Almighty has brought misfortune upon me."

BOOK OF RUTH 1:19–21 (NIV)

So they both went on until they came to Bethlehem. And when they arrived in Bethlehem, the whole town was stirred about them, and said, "Is this Naomi?"

And she said to them, Call me not Naomi [pleasant]; call me Mara [bitter], for the Almighty has dealt very bitterly with me.

I went out full, but the Lord has brought me home again empty. Why call me Naomi, since the Lord has testified against me, and the Almighty has afflicted me?"

BOOK OF RUTH 1:19–21 (TAB)

So they two went until they came to Bethlehem. And it came to pass, when they were come to Bethlehem, that all the city was moved about them, and they said, Is this Naomi?

And she said unto them, Call me not Naomi, call me Mara: for the Almighty hath dealt very bitterly with me.

I went out full and the LORD hath brought me home again empty: why then call ye me Naomi, seeing the LORD hath testified against me, and the Almighty hath afflicted me?

BOOK OF RUTH 1:19–21 (KJV)

One day Naomi her mother-in-law said to her, "My daughter, should I not try to find a home for you, where you will be well provided for? Is not Boaz, with whose servant girls you have been, a kinsman of ours? Tonight he will be winnowing barley on the threshing floor. Wash and perfume yourself, and put on your best clothes. Then go down to the threshing floor, but don't let him know you are there until he has finished eating and drinking. When he lies down, note the place where he is lying. Then go and uncover his feet and lie down. He will tell you what to do."

"I will do whatever you say," Ruth answered. So she went down to the threshing floor and did everything her mother-in-law told her to do.

BOOK OF RUTH 3:1–6 (NIV)

Then Naomi her mother-in-law said to Ruth, My daughter, shall I not seek rest or a home for you that you may prosper?

And now is not Boaz, with whose maidens you were, our relative? See, he is winnowing barley tonight at the threshing floor.

Wash and anoint yourself therefore, and put on your best clothes and go down to the threshing floor, but do not make yourself known to the man until he has finished eating and drinking.

But when he lies down, notice the place where he lies; then go and uncover his feet and lie down. And he will tell you what to do.

And Ruth said to her, All that you say to me I will do.

So she went down to the threshing floor and did just as her mother-in-law had told her.

BOOK OF RUTH 3:1–6 (TAB)

Then Naomi her mother in law said unto her, My daughter, shall I not seek rest for thee, that it may be well with thee?

And now is not Boaz of our kindred, with whose maidens thou wast? Behold, he winnoweth barley to night in the threshing floor.

Wash thyself therefore, and anoint thee, and put thy raiment upon thee, and get thee down to the floor: but make not thyself known unto the man, until he shall have done eating and drinking.

And it shall be, when he lieth down, that thou shalt mark the place where he shall lie, and thou shalt go in, and uncover his feet, and lay thee down; and he will tell thee what thou shalt do.

And she said unto her, all that thou sayest unto me I will do.

And she went down unto the floor, and did according to all that her mother in law bade her.

BOOK OF RUTH 3:1–6 (KJV)

Sarah

Age is Not a Factor

Abram and Nahor both married. The name of Abram's wife was Sarai, and the name of Nahor's wife was Milcah; she was the daughter of Haran, the father of both Milcah and Iscah. Now Sarai was barren; she had no children.

GENESIS 11:29–30 (NIV)

And Abram and Nahor took wives. The name of Abram's wife was Sarai, and the name of Nahor's wife was Milcah, the daughter of Haran the father of Milcah and Iscah. But Sarai was barren; she had no child.

GENESIS 11:29–30 (TAB)

And Abram and Nahor took them wives: the name of Abram's wife was Sarai; and the name of Nahor's wife, Milcah, the daughter of Haran, the father of Milcah, and the father of Iscah. But Sarai was barren; she had no child.

GENESIS 11:29–30 (KJV)

God also said to Abraham, "As for Sarai your wife, you are no longer to call her Sarai; her name will be Sarah. I will bless her and will surely give you a son by her. I will bless her so that she will be the mother of nations; kings of peoples will come from her."

GENESIS 17:15–16 (NIV)

And God said to Abraham; as for Sarai your wife, you shall not call her name Sarai; but Sarah [Princess] her name shall be.

And I will bless her and give you a son also by her. Yes, I will bless her, and she shall be a mother of nations; kings of peoples shall come from her.

GENESIS 17:15–16 (TAB)

And God said unto Abraham, as for Sarai thy wife, thou shalt not call her name Sarai, but Sarah shall her name be.

And I will bless her, and give thee a son also of her: yea, I will bless her, and she shall be a mother of nations; kings of people shall be of her.

GENESIS 17:15–16 (KJV)

"Where is your wife Sarah?" they asked him. "There, in the tent," he said.

Then the LORD said, "I will surely return to you about this time next year, and Sarah your wife will have a son."

Now Sarah was listening at the entrance to the tent, which was behind him. Abraham and Sarah were already old and well advanced in years, and Sarah was past the age of childbearing. So Sarah laughed to herself as she thought, "After I am worn out and my master is old, will I now have this pleasure?"

Then the LORD said to Abraham, "Why did Sarah laugh and say, 'Will I really have a child, now that I am old?' Is anything too hard for the LORD? I will return to you at the appointed time next year and Sarah will have a son."

GENESIS 18:9–14 (NIV)

And they said to him, Where is Sarah your wife? And he said, [She is here] in the tent.

[The Lord] said, I will surely return to you when the season comes round, and behold, Sarah your wife will have a son. And Sarah was listening and heard it at the tent door, which was behind Him.

Now Abraham and Sarah were old, well advanced in years; it had ceased to be with Sarah as with [young] women. [She was past the age of childbearing].

Therefore Sarah laughed to herself, saying, after I have become aged shall I have pleasure and delight, my Lord (husband), being old also?

And the Lord asked Abraham, Why did Sarah laugh, saying, Shall I really bear a child when I am so old?

Is anything too hard or too wonderful for the Lord? At the appointed time, when the season [for her delivery] comes around, I will return to you and Sarah shall have borne a son.

GENESIS 18:9–14 (TAB)

And they said unto him, Where is Sarah thy wife? And he said, Behold, in the tent.

And he said, I will certainly return unto thee according to the time of life; and, lo, Sarah thy wife shall have a son. And Sarah heard it in the tent door, which was behind him.

Now Abraham and Sarah were old and well stricken in age; and it ceased to be with Sarah after the manner of women.

Therefore Sarah laughed within herself, saying, after I am waxed old shall I have pleasure, my Lord being old also?

And the LORD said unto Abraham, Wherefore

did Sarah laugh, saying, Shall I of a surety bear a child, which am old?

Is any thing too hard for the LORD? At the time appointed I will return unto thee, according to the time of life, and Sarah shall have a son.

GENESIS 18:9–14 (KJV)

Now the LORD was gracious to Sarah as he had said, and the LORD did for Sarah what he had promised. Sarah became pregnant and bore a son to Abraham in his old age, at the very time God had promised him. Abraham gave the name Isaac to the son Sarah bore him. When his son Isaac was eight days old, Abraham circumcised him, as God commanded him. Abraham was a hundred years old when his son Isaac was born to him.

Sarah said, "God has brought me laughter, and everyone who hears about this will laugh with me." And she added, "Who would have said to Abraham that Sarah would nurse children? Yet I have borne him a son in his old age."

GENESIS 21:1–7 (NIV)

THE LORD visited Sarah as He had said, and the Lord did for her as He had promised.

For Sarah became pregnant and bore Abraham a son in his old age, at the set time God had told him.

Abraham named his son whom Sarah bore to him Isaac [laughter].

And Abraham circumcised his son Isaac when he was eight days old, as God had commanded him.

Abraham was a hundred years old when Isaac was born.

And Sarah said, God has made me to laugh; all who hear will laugh with me.

And she said, who would have said to Abraham that Sarah would nurse children at the breast? For I have borne him a son in his old age!

GENESIS 21:1–7 (TAB)

And the LORD visited Sarah as he had said, and the LORD did unto Sarah as he had spoken.

For Sarah conceived, and bare Abraham a son in his old age, at the set time of which God had spoken to him.

And Abraham called the name of his son that was born unto him, whom Sarah bare to him, Isaac.

And Abraham circumcised his son Isaac being eight days old, as God had commanded him.

And Abraham was an hundred years old, when his son Isaac was born unto him.

And Sarah said, God hath made me to laugh, so that all that hear will laugh with me.

And she said, who would have said unto Abraham, that Sarah should have given children suck? For I have born him a son in his old age.

GENESIS 21:1–7 (KJV)

Mary

Handmaiden of God

In the sixth month, God sent the angel Gabriel to Nazareth, a town in Galilee, to a virgin pledged to be married to a man named Joseph, a descendant of David. The virgin's name was Mary. The angel went to her and said, "Greetings, you who are highly favored! The Lord is with you." Mary was greatly troubled at his words and wondered what kind of greeting this might be. But the angel said to her, "Do not be afraid, Mary, you have found favor with God. You will be with child and give birth to a son, and you are to give him the name Jesus. He will be great and will be called the Son of the Most High. The Lord God will give him the throne of his father David, and he will reign over the house of Jacob forever; his kingdom will never end." "How will this be," Mary asked the angel, "since I am a virgin?"

The angel answered, "The Holy Spirit will come upon you, and the power of the Most High will overshadow you. So the holy one to be born will be called the Son of God. Even Elizabeth your relative is going to have a child in her old age, and she who was said to be barren is in her sixth month. For nothing is impossible with God." "I am the Lord's servant," Mary answered. "May it be to me as you have said." Then the angel left her.

LUKE 1:26–38 (NIV)

Now in the sixth month [after that], the angel Gabriel was sent from God to a town of Galilee named Nazareth,

To a girl never having been married and a virgin engaged to be married to a man whose name was Joseph, a descendant of the house of David; and the virgin's name was Mary.

And he came to her and said, Hail, O favored one [endued with grace]! The Lord is with you! Blessed (favored of God) are you before all other women!

But when she saw him, she was greatly troubled and disturbed and confused at what he said and kept revolving in her mind what such a greeting might mean.

And the angel said to her, Do not be afraid, Mary, for you have found grace (free, spontaneous, absolute favor and loving-kindness) with God.

And listen! You will become pregnant and will give birth to a Son, and you shall call His name Jesus.

He will be great (eminent) and will be called the Son of the Most High; and the Lord God will give to Him the throne of His forefather David,

And He will reign over the house of Jacob throughout the ages; and of His reign there will be no end.

And Mary said to the angel, how can this be, since I have no [intimacy with any man as a] husband?

Then the angel said to her, The Holy Spirit will come upon you, and the power of the Most High will overshadow you [like a shining cloud]; and so the holy (pure, sinless) Thing (Offspring), which shall be born of you, will be called the Son of God.

And listen! Your relative Elizabeth in her old age has also conceived a son, and this is now the sixth month with her who was called barren.

For with God nothing is ever impossible and no word from God shall be without power or impossible of fulfillment.

Then Mary said, Behold, I am the handmaiden of the Lord; let it be done to me according to what you have said. And the angel left her.

LUKE 1:26–38 (TAB)

And in the sixth month the angel Gabriel was sent from God unto a city of Galilee, named Nazareth,

To a virgin espoused to a man whose name was Joseph, of the house of David; and the virgin's name was Mary.

And the angel came in unto her, and said, Hail, thou that art highly favoured, the Lord is with thee: blessed art thou among women.

And when she saw him, she was troubled at his saying, and cast in her mind what manner of salutation this should be.

And the angel said unto her, Fear not, Mary: for thou hast found favour with God.

And, behold, thou shalt conceive in thy womb, and bring forth a son, and shalt call his name JESUS.

He shall be great, and shall be called the Son of the Highest: and the Lord God shall give unto him the throne of his father David: And he shall reign over the house of Jacob for ever; and of his kingdom there shall be no end.

Then said Mary unto the angel, How shall this be, seeing I know not a man?

And the angel answered and said unto her, The Holy Ghost shall come upon thee, and the power of the Highest shall overshadow thee: therefore also that holy thing which shall be born of thee shall be called the Son of God.

And, behold, thy cousin Elisabeth, she hath also conceived a son in her old age: and this is the sixth month with her, who was called barren.

For with God nothing shall be impossible.

And Mary said, Behold the handmaid of the Lord; be it unto me according to thy word. And the angel departed from her.

LUKE 1:26–38 (KJV)

At that time Mary got ready and hurried to a town in the hill country of Judea, where she entered Zechariah's home and greeted Elizabeth. When Elizabeth heard Mary's greeting, the baby leaped in her womb, and Elizabeth was filled with the Holy Spirit. In a loud voice she exclaimed: "Blessed are you among women, and blessed is the child you will bear! But why am I so favored, that the mother of my Lord should come to me? As soon as the sound of your greeting reached my ears, the baby in my womb leaped for joy. Blessed is she who has believed that what the Lord has said to her will be accomplished!"

LUKE 1:39–45 (NIV)

And at that time Mary arose and went with haste into the hill country to a town of Judah,

And she went to the house of Zachariah and, entering it, saluted Elizabeth.

And it occurred that when Elizabeth heard Mary's greeting, the baby leaped in her womb, and Elizabeth was filled with and controlled by the Holy Spirit.

And she cried out with a loud cry, and then exclaimed, Blessed (favored of God) above all other women are you! And blessed (favored of God) is the Fruit of your womb!

And how [have I deserved that this honor should] be granted to me, that the mother of my Lord should come to me?

For behold, the instant the sound of your salutation reached my ears, the baby in my womb leaped for joy.

And blessed (happy, to be envied) is she who

believed that there would be a fulfillment of the things that were spoken to her from the Lord.

LUKE 1:39–45 (TAB)

And Mary arose in those days, and went into the hill country with haste, into a city of Juda;

And entered into the house of Zachariah, and saluted Elisabeth.

And it came to pass, that, when Elisabeth heard the salutation of Mary, the babe leaped in her womb; and Elisabeth was filled with the Holy Ghost:

And she spake out with a loud voice, and said, Blessed art thou among women, and blessed is the fruit of thy womb.

And whence is this to me, that the mother of my Lord should come to me?

For, lo, as soon as the voice of thy salutation sounded in mine ears, the babe leaped in my womb for joy.

And blessed is she that believed: for there shall be a performance of those things which were told her from the Lord.

LUKE 1:39–45 (KJV)

Bibliography

Robertson, Pat. The Secret Kingdom: Your Path to Peace, Love and Financial
Security. Thomas Nelson; First edition (1982). Nashville, TN

Author's Note

If you are caught in an abusive relationship, I want to encourage you, first of all, that it is not your fault. Secondly, you do not deserve this kind of treatment from anyone. Thirdly, you can break free. God through his Son, Jesus Christ, died that you may be set free from the bondage of sin and walk in liberty. Jesus came that you may have life and have that life more abundantly.

So if this is where you are, and you would like to break free, the person of Jesus Christ is waiting for you.

Call the National Domestic Abuse Hotline–

800–799-SAFE (7233). There is someone on the other line who is there for you.

Domestic Violence

America's Growing Epidemic

Relationship abuse can happen to anyone regardless of race, age, sexual orientation, religion, gender, educational background, or social economic status.

It can be emotional abuse—violence with words.

It can be physical abuse—violence in which a person is physically injured or even killed.

Every twelve seconds a woman is beaten by her partner.

Fifty-two percent of female murder victims are killed by their partners.

More than half of Americans know some-one who has been involved in a violent relationship.

Domestic violence is the number one cause of emergency room visits by women.

Children from violent homes are seventy-four percent more likely to commit assault.

Ten Warning Signs of Abuse

These signs can save your life or the life of someone you love:

When your friend and her partner are together, he acts very controlling and puts her down in front of others.

He acts extremely jealous of others who pay attention to her, especially men.

She becomes quiet when he is around and seems afraid of making him angry.

She stops seeing her friends and family members, becoming more and more isolated.

He controls her finances, her behavior, and even those with whom she is allowed to socialize.

She often cancels plans at the last minute.

You see him violently lose his temper, striking or breaking objects.

She often has unexplained injuries, or the explanations don't add up. (You may not always see bruises, as batterers target their blows to areas that clothing covers.)

She has casually mentioned his violent
behavior but makes a joke out of it.
If she has children, they are frequently upset,
quiet, or withdrawn and won't say why.

Appendix

To help you get started on the road to Becoming a Woman God can Use, I have included a few sites that have been of some help to me.

Life Coaching
48 Days to the Work you Love
Dan Miller, Founder
P.O. Box 681381
Franklin, TN 37068–1381
(615) 373–7771
Web site: www.48days.com

Valorie Burton Inspire Inc.
1009 Bay Ridge Avenue #150
Annapolis, Maryland 21403
(410) 561–6041
Life Coach

Web site: www.valorieburton.com

Business Tools

Web site: http://www.irs.gov/businesses/index.html

Small Business Administration: Small Business Planner Web site: www.sba.gov/small/business-planner/index.html

You may also visit the Secretary of State Web site for your individual state to find local business resources.

Volunteer Opportunities
Web site: www.volunteermatch.org
To find local organizations in need of volunteers.

If you would like to correspond with Andrea or to schedule speaking engagements, you may contact her at:

Andrea Rose-Butler
PO Box 78
Hutto, Tx 78634
email: becomingwoman@newseasonsminitries.org
Web site: www.newseasonsministries.org